PENGUIN BOOKS

# CHARMAINE SOLOMON'S THAI COOKBOOK

Charmaine Solomon is one of the world's best known and most highly respected cookery writers, with twenty-eight cookbooks to her credit. Since her *Complete Asian Cookbook* was published in 1976, over a million copies have been sold, and it has been translated into German, French and Dutch.

With characteristic enthusiasm she declares: 'The *Thai Cookbook* is a particularly exciting project – it's wonderful food with the advantage of being both unusual and easy to prepare.' In 1995 Charmaine Solomon took yet another step towards bringing authentic Thai food within easy reach of all who appreciate good cooking. In the opening chapter of this book she provides recipes for curry pastes and, realising that many people do not have time to prepare them, she has produced a range of Thai curry pastes in Australia, marketed under her own name.

# Charmaine Solomon's

# THAI

# Cookbook

A Complete Guide to
the World's Most
Exciting Cuisine

PENGUIN BOOKS

PENGUIN BOOKS

Published by the Penguin Group
Penguin Books Ltd, 27 Wrights Lane, London W8 5TZ, England
Penguin Books USA Inc., 375 Hudson Street, New York, New York 10014, USA
Penguin Books Australia Ltd, Ringwood, Victoria, Australia
Penguin Books Canada Ltd, 10 Alcorn Avenue, Toronto, Ontario, Canada M4V 3B2
Penguin Books (NZ) Ltd, 182–190 Wairau Road, Auckland 10, New Zealand

Penguin Books Ltd, Registered Offices: Harmondsworth, Middlesex, England

First published in Australia by Greenhouse Publications 1989
This edition published in Australia by Viking 1996
Published in Penguin Books 1997
10 9 8 7 6 5 4 3 2 1

Food styling by Jill Pavey, Charmaine Solomon and Darlene Macklyn
Photography by Ray Joyce
Cover photography by Simon Griffiths
Front cover food styled by Louise Lechte

Typeset by Midland Typesetters, Maryborough, Victoria
Printed and bound in Australia by Australian Print Group, Maryborough, Victoria

# CONTENTS

# INTRODUCTION

*A*s in most great cuisines, there is, in Thailand, a classic cuisine and a peasant cuisine. Both are full of intriguing flavours. While everyday meals are down-to-earth, classic Thai cuisine is reminiscent of French *haute cuisine* – elaborate table arrangements, exquisitely detailed garnishes, the perfuming of food with herbs and even flowers. There is more romance in Thai cooking than any other cuisine in the world today.

Thai food is totally individual, befitting a country that has never been conquered, yet it has similarities to both Indian and Chinese food. From the former comes the use of fragrant spices in certain dishes. The Chinese influence shows in the use of noodles made from rice, wheat and bean starch. Their curved cooking pans, *ka-tha*, are just like the familiar wok, but often made in brass rather than steel. Because of the curved shape, very little oil is necessary, but ingredients must be kept constantly on the move and therefore the technique of stir-frying is as popular in Thai cooking as in Chinese cooking. Of course, you can use a frying pan but because it has a large, flat cooking surface it will be necessary to increase the amount of oil used.

Where soy sauce is indispensable in Chinese food, in Thai cooking it is fish sauce (*nam pla*). Thin, salty and not terribly fishy in spite of its name, it brings out other flavours and is added to every dish. If a more pronounced fish flavour is required, it is obtained from *kapi*, a paste made from shrimps, similar to the *blacan* of Malaysia and the *ngapi* of Burma.

Rice is the cornerstone of Thai cuisine. Every meal is built around a large amount of freshly cooked white rice. The best Thai rice is jasmine rice – white, long-grained, with a faint and delightful perfume. It is cooked without adding salt since the food that accompanies the rice is highly seasoned and salty. The rice is brought to the table in a covered bowl or individual woven baskets so it is kept steaming hot throughout the meal. In true Thai fashion, all the food is brought to the table at once and will include *khao* (rice), *kaeng* (dishes with gravy), *krueng kieng* (side dishes) and *kaeng chud* (soup).

In elegant Thai restaurants the meal is served in stages. First, two or more small appetisers with dipping sauces. Then the main course of rice accompanied by soup, curry, a fried dish, a steamed dish, a salad. When cooking at home and you wish to extend a meal to serve more people, make an extra dish or two and increase the amount of rice. Desserts are not usually a feature of Thai meals, some are eaten as snacks, others enjoyed as luscious, semi-liquid coolers between meals – an Asian habit which most people find liberating since it is quite legitimate, indeed necessary, to keep up one's energy.

If you get the impression I'm somewhat partial to Thai food and cooking, you're perfectly correct – it forms a considerable part of the meals I cook for my family. However, all the enthusiasm in the world doesn't ensure your busy schedule will allow you to start 'from scratch' each time. So I've arrived at ways to take the fuss and fiddle out of presenting a Thai meal. After all, there's no rule against making things easy.

If you shop for ingredients each time you want to cook Thai, chances are you'll do it far less frequently than you would like to. But if you convert those fresh ingredients into long-lasting supplies of curry pastes and store them in the refrigerator or freezer, preparation time is cut dramatically. No authenticity is lost using this system, and much as I enjoy cooking, there are other demands on my time and, I know, on yours too.

I wish you as much enjoyment in using this book as I have had in doing the research, preparing and tasting recipes, and trying to make it simple and rewarding to cook authentic, delicious Thai food in your own kitchen.

# CURRY PASTES AND OTHER BASIC FLAVOURS

*C*urry pastes are a basic in Thai cooking. Since they appear in many recipes, they are given a section of their own here, with suggestions on how to greatly cut down the time involved by making larger quantities than you need for a single dish. Most call for the essentials of coconut milk and cream, chillies, coriander and kaffir lime leaves and rind (see separate entries in the Glossary, page 205). If you're fond of Thai food and cook it often, having a supply of pastes is a great time saver. Refrigerate curry pastes in screw-top jars for up to four months and use as required, making sure you use a clean, dry spoon each time you take some from the jar. Return the jar to the refrigerator as soon as possible after use. Or, you may wish to freeze the paste in meal-size amounts to have ready whenever you have a yen for those incomparable flavours.

It is possible to purchase ready-made curry pastes, and while some of these are acceptable, the majority are inclined to be harsh. Those made in Asia may include monosodium glutamate, which many people prefer to do without. I have yet to find curry pastes as good and fresh-tasting as those made in the home from the recipes that follow. For dedicated cooks who prefer to make their own spice and herb blends, I have set out the formulas I use, preceded by recommendations on handling certain ingredients. Please note these carefully, they have been learned by sometimes painful trial and error!

I assure you that it is possible to cook Thai food with just a few basic saucepans, a frying pan, an ordinary wooden spoon and a colander. You can improvise a steamer with a large boiler, in which you place a trivet and then balance a cake rack. A frying pan will do the job of a wok; just be aware that it will require more oil, and it won't be as easy to stir-fry in.

In some cases I pass over the authentic article in everyday use. For example, my electric blender does the job faster than a mortar and pestle and with less effort on my part. But I sometimes pound away when only a small amount of something is required – the blender needs a fair quantity to work effectively. Some implements make certain tasks easier, so if you have a chance to browse in Asian stores, look for items which will be most useful to you. That, after all, is what this book is all about: delicious Thai food with no hassles.

# RED CURRY PASTE

*Kruang Kaeng Dang* (Makes about 1 cup/8 fl oz)

10 fresh or dried hot red
   chillies, seeded
½ cup small purple shallots or
   2 small brown onions,
   chopped
1 tablespoon chopped garlic
¼ cup finely sliced lemon
   grass or zest of 1 lemon
1 tablespoon chopped
   galangal, fresh or bottled or
   3 teaspoons powdered
   galangal
1 tablespoon chopped fresh
   coriander roots
1 tablespoon chopped fresh
   coriander stems
1 teaspoon finely grated kaffir
   lime rind
4 kaffir lime leaves, mid-ribs
   removed
2 tablespoons peanut oil
2 teaspoons dried shrimp
   paste
1 tablespoon coriander seeds
2 teaspoons cummin seeds
1 teaspoon black peppercorns
2 teaspoons paprika
1 teaspoon ground turmeric

1 In the container of an electric blender put the chillies, shallots, garlic, lemon grass, galangal, coriander roots and stems, lime rind and the lime leaves. Add the oil and blend to a smooth purée.

2 Wrap the shrimp paste closely in foil and flatten to make a small packet. Place under a hot griller (broiler) and cook for 2 to 3 minutes on each side.

3 In a small saucepan toast the coriander seeds until golden and fragrant, then turn onto a plate. Toast the cummin seeds until fragrant. Lightly toast the peppercorns also, and grind all three to a powder in a mortar and pestle. Add to the blender with the paprika, ground turmeric and shrimp paste. Blend once more.

4 Store in a clean, dry bottle in the refrigerator for 3–4 months, or divide into convenient portions, wrap and freeze.

# GREEN CURRY PASTE

*Kruang Kaeng Khiew Wan* (Makes about 1 cup/8 fl oz)

*Don't let the colour fool you, a green curry can be devastatingly hot if prepared the traditional way. For less heat, discard the chilli seeds.*

4 large or 8 small green
   chillies, seeded
½ cup purple shallots or
   1 medium onion, chopped
1 tablespoon chopped garlic
½ cup chopped fresh
   coriander, including roots,
   stems and leaves
¼ cup finely sliced lemon
   grass or zest of 1 lemon
1 tablespoon chopped
   galangal, fresh or bottled
2 teaspoons ground coriander
1 teaspoon ground cumin
1 teaspoon black peppercorns
1 teaspoon ground turmeric
1 teaspoon dried shrimp paste
2 tablespoons peanut oil

1 Remove the stems and roughly chop the chillies. Put into an electric blender with all the other ingredients and blend to a smooth paste. Add a tablespoon of extra oil or a little water if necessary to facilitate blending.

2 Store in a clean, dry bottle in the refrigerator for 3–4 months, or divide into convenient portions, wrap and freeze.

# MASAMAN (MUSLIM) CURRY PASTE

*Kruang Kaeng Masaman* (Makes about ¾ cup/6 fl oz)

*Influenced by the Muslims from India, as evidenced by the use of fragrant spices.*

7–10 dried red chillies or
   2 teaspoons chilli powder
2 tablespoons peanut oil
2 medium onions, chopped
1 tablespoon chopped garlic
1 teaspoon dried shrimp paste
2 teaspoons finely chopped
   lemon grass or lemon zest
1 tablespoon chopped
   galangal or 2 teaspoons
   powdered galangal
2 tablespoons coriander seeds
   or ground coriander
2 teaspoons cummin seeds or
   ground cummin
1 teaspoon fennel seeds or
   ground fennel
1 teaspoon ground cinnamon
½ teaspoon ground cardamom
½ teaspoon ground nutmeg or
   mace
¼ teaspoon ground cloves

1  Break the chillies, shake out the seeds and soak the chillies in boiling water for 10–15 minutes.

2  Heat the oil and fry the onions and garlic over low heat until they are soft and start turning brown. Add the shrimp paste and fry for a minute longer, crushing it in the oil with the back of a spoon.

3  Remove from the heat and when cool put the mixture into the container of an electric blender with the soaked and drained chillies, lemon grass and galangal. Blend to a smooth purée, adding a little water if necessary to facilitate blending.

4  In a dry pan roast the coriander seeds until brown, shaking the pan or stirring frequently. Turn out and allow to cool while roasting the cummin and fennel seeds slightly.

5  Pound all the seeds in a mortar and pestle to a fine powder. If using ground coriander, cummin and fennel, they may be combined and dry-roasted in a small pan, using low heat and stirring constantly to ensure they do not burn. Roast until they are a rich brown colour and have a fine aromatic smell.

6  Combine with the puréed ingredients, and add the ground cinnamon, cardamom, nutmeg and cloves.

7  Store in a clean, dry bottle in the refrigerator for 3–4 months or divide into convenient portions, wrap and freeze.

# HOT AND SOUR SOUP PASTE

Tom Yum *paste* *(Makes about 1½ cups/12 fl oz)*

*Although basically a flavouring for the tongue-tingling* tom yum *soups made with prawns, chicken or other main ingredients, this is a wonderful flavouring for other dishes too. I feel lost without a constant supply of it in the refrigerator.*

*To make a soup for 4 people, use 1–2 tablespoons of this paste, 250 g (8 oz) chicken or prawns (shrimp) and 3 cups (24 fl oz) stock. Add extra fresh lime juice to accentuate the refreshingly sour flavour.*

½ cup (4 fl oz) vegetable oil
2 teaspoons chilli powder
1 tablespoon water
½ cup dried shrimp
½ cup finely sliced lemon
   grass or zest of 1 lemon
1 tablespoon finely chopped
   garlic
2 tablespoons chopped
   coriander roots
10 whole peppercorns
1 tablespoon finely chopped
   galangal or 2 teaspoons
   dried galangal powder
4 fresh red chillies, seeded
4 fresh green chillies, seeded
8 fresh, frozen or dried kaffir
   lime leaves (soaked if they
   are dried)
4 tablespoons (3 fl oz) fish
   sauce
4 tablespoons (3 fl oz) lime
   juice
1 teaspoon ground turmeric
1 tablespoon dried shrimp
   paste
1 tablespoon salt
1 tablespoon sugar
1 tablespoon citric acid
1 teaspoon finely grated lime
   rind

1 Pour the oil into a warm wok or frying pan and on low heat, add the chilli powder mixed with the water and cook, stirring, until the oil turns red.

2 In an electric blender reduce the dried shrimp to a floss and empty into a bowl.

3 Put the lemon grass, garlic, coriander, peppercorns, galangal, fresh chillies and kaffir lime leaves into the electric blender with the fish sauce and lime juice, and blend at high speed to a smooth purée.

4 Add to the wok together with the turmeric, shrimp paste and shrimp floss and cook, stirring frequently, until the oil comes to the surface. Cool, stir in the salt, sugar, citric acid and lime rind.

5 Store tightly covered in a clean, dry glass bottle in the refrigerator for 3–4 months; or freeze in 1 or 2 tablespoon amounts for longer periods.

# PANANG CURRY PASTE

*Kruang Kaeng Panang* (Makes about 1½ cups/12 fl oz)

10 long dried chillies
½ cup (4 fl oz) hot water
1 teaspoon grated kaffir lime
   rind
4 slices galangal, fresh or
   bottled
½ cup chopped shallots or
   spring onions
2 stalks lemon grass, finely
   sliced or zest of 1 lemon
1 tablespoon chopped garlic
8 fresh coriander roots,
   chopped
1 tablespoon whole black
   peppercorns
2 teaspoons shrimp paste
1 tablespoon fish sauce
2 teaspoons salt
½ cup (4 oz) crunchy peanut
   butter
⅓ cup (2½ fl oz) peanut oil

1 Break open the chillies, discard the stems and seeds, and soak the chillies in hot water for 15 minutes. Put the chillies with the soaking water and all the remaining ingredients, except the peanut butter and oil, into an electric blender and blend to a smooth purée.

2 Stir in the peanut butter and oil, bottle and store in the refrigerator for 3–4 months. Use about 3 tablespoons of this curry paste to each 500 g (1 lb) meat or poultry.

# PEPPER AND CORIANDER PASTE

*Rark Pak Chee, Prik Thai* (Makes about 1 cup/8 fl oz)

*These are such basic flavourings for Thai food that I find this recipe saves a great deal of the time spent making the mixture each time it is needed. It takes almost as long to make a small quantity as a large one, so store some in a glass jar in the refrigerator in readiness for your adventures in Thai cooking. So far I have not come across this mixture bottled commercially.*

**1 tablespoon chopped garlic**
**2 teaspoons salt**
**2 tablespoons whole black peppercorns**
**2 cups well-washed, coarsely chopped fresh coriander including roots**
**2 tablespoons lemon juice**

NOTE *This paste may also be made in a blender, but in this case reduce the black peppercorns to 1 tablespoon because it is hotter if finely ground than if coarsely crushed.*

1 Crush the garlic with the salt to a smooth paste.

2 Roast the peppercorns in a dry pan for a minute or two, then coarsely crush in a mortar and pestle.

3 Finely chop the coriander roots, leaves and stems. Mix all the ingredients together, adding the lemon juice.

4 Store in a clean, dry bottle in the refrigerator for 3–4 months, or divide into convenient portions, wrap and freeze.

# APPETISERS AND SAVOURY SNACKS

*A*ppetisers and savouries are very important in Thai cuisine. People love these small morsels sold on the streets, served at parties, or eaten between meals. While there are no 'courses' as there are in a Western meal, these snacks could easily be described as *hors d'oeuvres*, meaning 'outside the menu'. Some are fairly substantial two-bite or three-bite morsels, but most are very dainty. All are readily classified as finger food.

The range of Thai appetisers and savoury snacks, as you can see, is fascinating. Some are wrapped in edible leaves, others in leaves that flavour the food but are then discarded. Some are savoury mixtures folded in paper-thin, transparent dough; others are served in hollowed-out fruit or water chestnuts.

In Thailand, extra seasonings come in many forms: salt, sugar, crushed roasted peanuts or sesame seeds – handy for those who eat on the run. But when eating at the table, as people do at road-side food stalls at all hours of the day and night, many snacks come with their own dipping sauces.

Everything is so pretty, and titbits that will vanish in a single mouthful are still presented with incredibly detailed decoration.

# FRESH SPRING ROLLS

*Poh Pia* (Makes 8)

*These are fresh spring rolls, the rice-paper wrapping pliable and transparent instead of crisp-fried and golden brown – an ideal low-fat version of the popular snack.*

CLEAR SAUCE
4 tablespoons sugar
½ cup (4 fl oz) cold water
2 tablespoons fish sauce
finely sliced red and green
   chillies, seeded
1 tablespoon lime juice or
   vinegar

FILLING
½ cup dried shrimp
1 cup soaked fine rice
   noodles, drained
1 or 2 sliced chillies
2 teaspoons fish sauce
1 teaspoon lime juice or
   vinegar
1 teaspoon sugar
1 tablespoon shredded dried
   radish
8 round rice-paper sheets
16 small cooked prawns
   (shrimp), shelled and
   deveined
about 48 basil leaves
8 small pieces of lettuce
lettuce leaves (garnish)
shredded carrot and white
   radish (garnish)

1  **TO MAKE THE CLEAR SAUCE,** stir the sugar and cold water until the sugar dissolves, then add the remaining ingredients.

2  **TO MAKE THE FILLING,** soak the dried shrimp in hot water for 10 minutes, then drain and chop.

3  Measure out the fine rice noodles after soaking them in hot water for 10 minutes. Drain well and chop into short lengths. Mix the shrimp and noodles with the chillies, fish sauce, lime juice and sugar. Simmer the shredded radish in water for 5 minutes, drain and add to the mixture.

4  Dip a sheet of rice paper in warm water until pliable and lay on a flat surface. Place 2 prawns on one side of the rice paper and then a heaped tablespoon of the noodle mixture. Cover with about 6 basil leaves and a small piece of lettuce. Bring the ends of the rice paper together and roll up, enclosing the filling firmly.

5  Arrange on the lettuce leaves with the prawns showing through on top and the seam underneath. Garnish with fine shreds of carrot and white radish, and serve with the Clear Sauce.

# LEAF LILIES

*Miang Cha Plu (Makes about 30)*

*The leaf known as* cha plu *(Piper sarmentosum) is an attractive, glossy leaf with a tangy flavour. It is filled with tasty mixtures and sold as a snack. If the leaves are soaked in water with a little sugar added to keep them in good condition, I have discovered that not only do they stay fresh, they also take on a slightly sweet and most pleasant flavour. You can substitute butter lettuce or any other pliable leaf that can be eaten without cooking.*

1 bunch *cha plu* leaves or
   1 butter lettuce
2 teaspoons Red Curry Paste
   (*page 3*)
2 tablespoons coconut milk
2 tablespoons chopped spring
   onions
90 g (3 oz) minced (ground)
   pork
60 g (2 oz) flaked, cooked crab
   meat
1 tablespoon finely chopped
   coriander leaves
1 tablespoon crushed, roasted
   peanuts
1 teaspoon palm sugar
1 teaspoon chopped red chilli,
   seeded
½ cup cold cooked rice
1 teaspoon finely chopped
   kaffir lime leaves (garnish)
a few fine strips of red chillies
   (garnish)

---

NOTE *If preferred, fill the leaves with a mixture of toasted coconut and dried shrimp pounded together and moistened with lime juice. Top with crushed roasted peanuts, finely chopped fresh ginger and small shallots, a little sugar and some sliced fresh, hot chilli.*

---

1 Wash the *cha plu* leaves and soak for at least 2 hours in cold water with a couple of spoonfuls of sugar dissolved in it. The leaves may be soaked overnight.

2 Heat the Red Curry Paste and coconut milk together, stirring. Add the spring onions and pork, and stir-fry until the pork is cooked. Remove from heat and mix in the crab meat, coriander leaves, crushed peanuts, palm sugar, chopped chilli and rice.

3 Drain the *cha plu* leaves, blot dry on a clean tea towel and place a spoonful of the mixture near the stem. Roll each into a lily shape and fasten at the base with a toothpick. Garnish with lime leaves and chilli strips. Serve with a dipping sauce.

4 To eat remove the toothpick, fold the lily into a little parcel, and serve with a dipping sauce if desired.

# GOLDEN CUPS

*Krathong Tong* (Makes about 30)

*The crisp, light batter in a flower shape holds a savoury mixture and is named for the lotus-shaped floats that are so much a part of the* Loy Krathong *festival, the biggest celebration of the year in Thailand.*

*You will need to prepare a special* krathong *mould or improvise one. The mould is a fluted metal shape attached to a wooden handle. I find a fluted tartlet tin grasped firmly with metal tongs works very well as an alternative. See colour plate on page 25.*

## FILLING
1 clove garlic
2 coriander roots
1 small onion, chopped
1 tablespoon peanut oil
125 g (4 oz) minced (ground)
  pork or chicken
1 red chilli, sliced
2 spring onions, finely
  chopped
1 tablespoon chopped pickled
  garlic
2 teaspoons fish sauce
1 teaspoon palm sugar
1 tablespoon lime juice
1 tablespoon crushed, roasted
  peanuts
fresh coriander leaves
  (garnish)
2 tablespoons corn kernels
  (garnish)

## BATTER
¼ cup (1 oz) rice flour
¼ cup (1 oz) plain (all-
  purpose) flour
¼ cup (2 fl oz) canned
  coconut milk
¼ cup (2 fl oz) water
1 teaspoon sugar
peanut oil for deep-frying

---

NOTE *The cups may be made ahead and stored in an airtight container when completely cold.*

---

1 **TO MAKE THE FILLING**, pound the garlic, coriander roots and onion together. Heat the oil and fry the mixture on gentle heat until it is fragrant and starts to turn golden.

2 Add the meat and fry, stirring until it changes colour. Add the remaining ingredients except for the garnish and continue to cook, stirring frequently, for 10 minutes. Leave to cool to room temperature before using.

3 **TO MAKE THE BATTER**, combine the flours with the coconut milk and water, stirring to a thick, smooth batter. If necessary, add an extra tablespoon of water to give a batter that will coat the mould. Stir in the sugar.

4 Heat the oil for deep-frying in a small pan. Dip the mould in the oil, lift out and let the oil drain for a second or two. Dip it into the batter, being careful not to immerse the top of the mould or the batter will not detach from it. Return the mould to the oil and hold it till the cup is golden and floats free. Lift from the oil onto absorbent paper when golden.

5 For maximum crispness, fill the cups just before serving. Garnish with coriander leaves and corn kernels.

# DEEP-FRIED CURRY PUFFS

*Kari Puff (Makes about 20)*

*The weekend market in Bangkok is an experience no visitor should miss. There they were selling curry puffs so tiny that I wondered at the fact each still had a perfect rope edge decoration. One small mouthful, nothing more. We tried making them this size. It is possible, but it's easier when they are just a little larger. The curry puffs can be made ahead and frozen for up to 2 months. See colour plate on page 25.*

## FILLING
1 tablespoon peanut oil
2 teaspoons finely chopped
    coriander roots
2 teaspoons finely chopped
    garlic
500 g (1 lb) minced (ground)
    beef or pork
3 tablespoons fish sauce
¼ teaspoon ground black
    pepper
1 teaspoon ground turmeric
1 teaspoon ground cummin
2 teaspoons ground coriander
1 hot chilli, seeded and finely
    chopped (optional)
½ cup raw potato, cut into
    6 mm (¼ in) dice
2 teaspoons sugar

## PASTRY
2 cups (8 oz) plain (all-
    purpose) flour
½ teaspoon salt
60 g (2 oz) butter
¼ cup (2 fl oz) coconut milk
peanut oil for deep-frying

NOTE *To freeze uncooked curry puffs, arrange them on a baking tray (not touching) and freeze until firm. Pack into freezer bags, extract the air and return to the freezer. To thaw, arrange them on a tray lined with absorbent paper and cover with more paper to absorb the excess moisture.*

1 **TO MAKE THE FILLING**, heat the oil in a wok or frying pan and cook the coriander roots and garlic over gentle heat until golden. Add the beef or pork, raise the heat to medium-high and stir-fry until it changes colour. Add the fish sauce, pepper, turmeric, cummin and coriander, and stir well. Cover and cook on low heat for 25 minutes, or until the meat is tender and the liquid is reduced.

2 Stir in the chilli if using, potatoes and sugar, cover and cook for another 10 minutes. The potatoes should still be firm. If necessary, cook uncovered for the final few minutes so the liquid evaporates completely. Remove from the heat and allow to cool.

3 **TO MAKE THE PASTRY**, sift the flour and salt, rub in the butter and add sufficient coconut milk to make a fairly firm dough. Form into a ball and knead lightly on a floured board until smooth. Wrap in plastic film and chill for at least 30 minutes.

4 On a floured surface roll out the pastry to about 3 mm (⅛ in) thickness. Cut into 10 cm (4 in) circles and brush the edges with cold water. Place a tablespoon of the cooled filling on each circle slightly below the centre. Bring the pastry over the filling and press the edges together to seal.

5 To make the rope edge, fold over one corner of the pastry at a 45-degree angle and press it flat. Then fold over the next section to make a rough triangle over the first fold. Repeat around the edge of the pastry, pressing each fold as you go.

6 Heat the oil for deep-frying and fry a few puffs at a time until golden brown. The oil should be hot enough to cook them in a couple of minutes. If the oil is not hot enough, the pastry will be heavy and oily instead of crisp and light. Drain on absorbent paper and serve warm or at room temperature.

# STEAMED DUMPLINGS WITH PORK AND CHICKEN

*Khanom Jeeb (Makes about 20)*

*These pitcher-shaped dumplings should be small enough to eat in one mouthful. Season the filling well so it is not neutralised by the blandness of the dough. A popular garnish and flavour accent is added by sprinkling the dumplings with crushed fried garlic (page 208) just before serving. Serve extra garlic separately, for those who wish to indulge.*

**DOUGH**
1 cup (4 oz) rice flour
¼ cup (1 oz) tapioca flour
¼ teaspoon salt
2 tablespoons peanut oil
1 cup (8 fl oz) water

**FILLING**
125 g (4 oz) minced (ground) pork
250 g (8 oz) chicken fillets, minced (ground)
3 tablespoons peanut oil
1 medium onion, finely chopped
1 tablespoon Pepper and Coriander Paste (*page 8*)
or 2 teaspoons finely chopped garlic
   2 tablespoons finely chopped fresh coriander, including roots
   ½ teaspoon black peppercorns, crushed
2 or 3 small hot chillies, seeded and finely chopped
1 tablespoon fish sauce
1 tablespoon palm sugar
3 tablespoons roasted, salted peanuts, crushed
red chilli slices (garnish)
fried garlic (optional)

**1 TO MAKE THE DOUGH,** combine the rice and tapioca flours, salt, oil and water in a saucepan and stir over moderate heat until it becomes a paste. Turn it into a bowl and when cool enough to handle, knead to a smooth paste. Divide it into 20 small balls, and cover with a damp cloth. Leave aside while preparing the filling.

**2 TO MAKE THE FILLING,** combine the pork and chicken. Heat the oil and fry the onion, stirring frequently, until it softens. Add the Pepper and Coriander Paste or the garlic, coriander and peppercorns. Stir-fry until fragrant.

**3** Add the pork and chicken and stir to break up any lumps. Keep frying until the meats are well cooked, then add the chillies, fish sauce and palm sugar. Stir constantly until the liquid has evaporated. Turn onto a plate to cool and mix in the peanuts.

**4** With floured hands, mould the balls of the dough into small cup shapes. Place a teaspoonful of filling inside each and gather the edges together to seal. Pinch off any excess dough and flatten the top of each dumpling. Using a fine metal skewer, mark with lines all round to decorate. Place on oiled greaseproof paper and steam for 20 minutes. After 5 minutes, lift the dumplings onto the serving plate and garnish each one with a slice of red chilli. Serve with crushed fried garlic, if desired.

# STEAMED PORK DUMPLINGS

*Khanom Jeeb Moo (Makes about 24)*

**FILLING**
1 tablespoon peanut oil
1 large onion, finely chopped
2 teaspoons Pepper and
  Coriander Paste (*page 8*)
500 g (1 lb) minced (ground)
  pork
3 teaspoons palm sugar
2 tablespoons fish sauce
½ cup (2 oz) crushed, roasted
  peanuts
roasted peanuts, crushed or
  fried garlic flakes, crushed
  (garnish)

**DOUGH**
1 cup (4 oz) gluten-free flour
  (wheat starch)
3 tablespoons cornflour
  (cornstarch)
¾ cup (6 fl oz) boiling water
1 tablespoon peanut oil
¼ teaspoon salt

---

**NOTE** *Fried garlic is most easily made by frying some dried garlic flakes on gentle heat. These burn easily, so lift them out as soon as they turn pale golden. Drain on absorbent paper and when cool and crisp, crush lightly.*

**1 TO MAKE THE FILLING,** heat the oil and stir-fry the onion until soft. Add the Pepper and Coriander Paste and cook until fragrant.

**2** Add the minced pork and cook, stirring, for 10–15 minutes or until it changes colour. Add the sugar, fish sauce and peanuts and cool before filling the dumplings.

**3 TO MAKE THE DOUGH,** sift the flours into a bowl. In a small saucepan bring the water to the boil. Add the oil and salt and pour onto the flour, stirring constantly with a wooden spoon. When cool enough to handle, knead lightly until smooth.

**4** Shape the dough into a cylinder about 2.5 cm (1 in) in diameter and divide into 1 cm (½ in) slices. Wrap in plastic film to prevent the surface from drying out.

**5** Take a piece of dough and roll out to a circle 8 cm (3 in) in diameter. Moisten one edge with water. Place 1 teaspoonful of pork mixture in the centre and fold over. Pinch the edges of the dough together decoratively.

**6** Place the dumplings on a lightly oiled plate and steam until the dough is transparent, about 15–20 minutes. Sprinkle with extra crushed peanuts or crushed fried garlic and serve hot with a salad.

# PORK-FILLED SAGO BALLS

*Saku Sai Moo* (Makes about 60 balls)

*These glistening, translucent little mouthfuls are not only pretty to look at but wonderfully savoury to eat. Serve as an appetiser with pre-dinner drinks or put them on the table as a preliminary to the main dishes. If the recipe makes more than required, the extras may be frozen and steamed when needed.*

1½ cups (8 oz) sago
¾ cup (6 fl oz) hot water
¼ teaspoon salt

FILLING
2 coriander plants
3 large cloves garlic
½ teaspoon whole black
    peppercorns or 2 teaspoons
    Pepper and Coriander Paste
    (*page 8*)
2 tablespoons peanut oil
1 medium onion, finely
    chopped
250 g (8 oz) lean minced
    (ground) pork
3 teaspoons palm sugar or
    brown sugar
2 tablespoons fish sauce
⅓ cup crushed, roasted
    peanuts or crunchy peanut
    butter
½ cup (2 oz) tapioca flour
2 teaspoons crisp-fried garlic
    flakes, crushed or roasted
    peanuts, crushed
chilli flowers

1  Rinse the sago in a fine strainer, transfer to a bowl and gradually mix in the hot water in which the salt has been dissolved. Mix well, cover and stand for an hour.

2  **TO MAKE THE FILLING**, roughly chop the coriander roots and stems and the garlic. Pound to a paste in a mortar and pestle, then transfer to a plate. Pound the black peppercorns until coarsely crushed.

3  Heat the oil in a wok or frying pan and cook the coriander-garlic paste and onion over low heat until soft. Add the peppercorns or Pepper and Coriander Paste, and cook until the mixture starts to brown.

4  Add the pork, increase the heat and fry, pressing the meat with the back of the spatula to prevent lumping. Cook until browned. Reduce the heat to medium, add the palm sugar and fish sauce and stir well. Cover and cook on low heat until the pork is tender and the liquid is all absorbed. Stir frequently to ensure the mixture doesn't stick and burn. Remove from the heat, stir in the peanuts or peanut butter, and allow to cool slightly.

5  With a wet teaspoon, take small amounts of sago and roll into balls with damp hands. Cover with a damp cloth.

6  Wash and dry your hands and dust with tapioca flour. Hollow out each ball into a cup shape, put in small teaspoonfuls of pork mixture and seal the sago over the filling. Mould into balls again and set aside, covered. Continue until all the filling is used.

7  Place the balls on oiled paper strips in a steamer, leaving some space between as they increase slightly in size. Steam over fast-boiling water for 15–20 minutes or until the sago is quite clear. Remove the steamer from the heat and allow to stand for about 5 minutes for the balls to dry slightly before transferring to the serving dish. Sprinkle with crushed fried garlic or roasted peanuts, and garnish with chilli flowers. Serve hot.

# FAT HORSES

*Ma Uon* (Makes about 16)

*I suppose these may be described as bite-sized terrines steamed in tiny moulds. If possible, shape cups from banana leaves but, more realistically, use foil confectionery cups or the small wine cups sold in Asian supermarkets.*

125 g (4 oz) minced (ground)
  pork
125 g (4 oz) chicken thigh
  fillets, skin removed and
  diced
125 g (4 oz) cooked and
  flaked crab meat
2 tablespoons freshly chopped
  coriander, including roots
¼ teaspoon ground black
  pepper
2 teaspoons chopped garlic
2 tablespoons finely chopped
  spring onions
2 tablespoons fish sauce
2 tablespoons thick coconut
  milk
2 small eggs
2 red chillies, sliced (garnish)
fresh coriander leaves
  (garnish)

1 Put the pork and chicken into a food processor. Pick over the crab meat and discard any bits of cartilage or shell.

2 Pound the fresh coriander, pepper and garlic to a paste. Add to the meats and process until smooth.

3 Transfer to a bowl and mix in the crab meat, spring onions, fish sauce and coconut milk.

4 Beat one egg and the white of the second egg together and add to the mixture. Press into small cups, smoothing the tops. Stir the yolk of the second egg and brush the tops with it.

5 Steam over boiling water for 20 minutes, cool and remove from the cups. Garnish each with a slice of chilli and a couple of coriander leaves before serving.

# GALLOPING HORSES (FRUIT WITH SAVOURY TOPPING)

*Ma Ho* *(Makes about 24)*

*It's a curious name, but so well known that if you're ordering in a Thai restaurant this is what you should ask for. Or go one better and use its Thai name – Ma ho.*

250 g (8 oz) minced (ground) pork or pork chop
2 teaspoons finely chopped garlic
1 tablespoon chopped fresh coriander roots
¼ teaspoon black pepper
2 tablespoons peanut oil
¼ cup (1 oz) roasted peanuts, crushed
1–2 tablespoons fish sauce
3 tablespoons palm sugar
1 fresh red chilli, seeded and chopped
2 tablespoons freshly chopped coriander leaves and stems
approximately 24 orange or mandarin segments

1 If using a pork chop, trim off the skin and bone, and chop the meat very finely. Pound the garlic, coriander roots and black pepper together in a mortar and pestle or, if you have some already made up, use a tablespoon of Pepper and Coriander Paste (*page 8*).

2 Heat the oil in a wok or frying pan and cook the mixture on low heat until it smells fragrant. Add the pork and fry until it changes colour. Add the peanuts, fish sauce, palm sugar, chilli and coriander and continue to stir-fry until the mixture is well cooked, dark brown and quite dry.

3 Segment the oranges or mandarins. Slit through the membrane and flesh and open the segments flat, removing any seeds. Place a spoonful of pork on each piece of fruit. Thin slices of pineapple may be used instead if convenient.

# PORK-STUFFED CAPSICUM IN EGG NET

*Prik Sod Sai Rum* (Makes 4)

*An appetiser on its own, or as part of the range of accompaniments served with Iced Rice (page 171).*

2 eggs
1 tablespoon water
¼ teaspoon salt
2 tablespoons dried shrimp or
    60 g (2 oz) fresh prawns
    (shrimp)
1 tablespoon Pepper and
    Coriander Paste (*page 8*)
1 teaspoon finely chopped
    garlic
1 tablespoon fish sauce
1 teaspoon palm sugar
125 g (4 oz) minced (ground)
    pork
4 banana capsicums (bell
    peppers)

1 **TO MAKE THE EGG NETS,** beat the eggs, water and salt together. Puncture several fine holes in the base of a clean empty can or plastic food container. Lightly grease a heated wok or frying pan. Fill the can with the egg mixture and make quick criss-crossing actions over the base of the pan to form a net. Use low heat because the egg net should not become brown. When set, loosen the net with a spatula or knife, then carefully lift off and place on a plate. Repeat with the remaining mixture. Leave the nets to cool before using.

2 If using dried shrimp, soak in hot water for 10 minutes, then drain and chop. Pound the prawns, Pepper and Coriander Paste, garlic, fish sauce and palm sugar, or chop in a food processor. Add to the pork mince and mix well.

3 Cut the stem end off each capsicum and with a pointed knife carefully remove all the seeds. Pack with the pork mixture, using a small spoon. Replace the stem end and steam for 10–15 minutes. Allow to cool for a few minutes, wrap with the egg nets, and serve with Chilli Sauce (*page 54*) and Chilli and Cucumber Salad (*page 60*).

# STUFFED STEAMED MUSSELS

*Hoi Mangpoo Mok* (*Serves 4*)

*If preferred, use 125 g (4 oz) fish fillets or prawn meat instead of the pork to make the savoury topping for the mussels.*

500 g (1 lb) small mussels
125 g (4 oz) minced (ground)
    pork
2 teaspoons Pepper and
    Coriander Paste (*page 8*) or
    Red Curry Paste (*page 3*)
1 tablespoon finely chopped
    lemon grass or zest of
    1 lemon
½ teaspoon grated kaffir lime
    rind
2 tablespoons thinly sliced
    spring onions
2 teaspoons cornflour
    (cornstarch)
2 teaspoons fish sauce
1 teaspoon palm sugar
1 egg white
kaffir lime leaf, finely
    shredded
red chilli, finely shredded

1  Scrub the mussels well with a brush under cold water. Beard the mussels by giving a sharp tug at the brown fibres protruding from the shells. The mussel shells should be tightly shut – discard any which are not. Place the mussels on a rack and steam until the shells open, discarding any which remain closed. Remove the top shells and discard.

2  Combine the pork and the next eight ingredients, mixing well. Top each mussel with a heaped teaspoon of the mixture, smoothing it over the mussel. Place fine shreds of lime leaf and chilli on each and arrange in a steamer.

3  Steam over boiling water for 15 minutes, or until cooked and firm. Serve warm or cold.

# STEAMED FISH PUDDING

*Hor Mok Pla* (Serves 6)

*This steamed fish pudding may be cooked in one large dish instead of individual cups, in which case it will need 25–30 minutes cooking time.*

12 × 15 cm (6 in) diameter
   circles of double foil or
   banana leaf
500 g (1 lb) white fish fillets
1½ cup (12 fl oz) thick
   coconut milk
2 tablespoons Red Curry Paste
   (*page 3*)
2 eggs, lightly beaten
1 tablespoon fish sauce
1 teaspoon salt
1 teaspoon finely chopped
   *krachai* (*page 208*)
   (optional)
1 teaspoon shrimp paste
1 cup basil leaves, tightly
   packed
3 teaspoons rice flour
1 or 2 kaffir lime leaves, very
   finely shredded
2 red chillies, seeded and
   finely sliced
12 fresh coriander leaves
   (garnish)

1 **TO MAKE THE CUPS** to hold the fish puddings, make 4 evenly spaced folds around the diameter of the foil or banana leaf. Fasten each fold with staples or toothpicks.

2 Clean the fish very carefully so it is free of all bones and skin. Process the fish to a purée in a food processor or chop it finely. Mix ¾ cup (6 fl oz) of the coconut milk with the Red Curry Paste and knead well with the fish. Stir in the eggs, fish sauce, salt, *krachai* and shrimp paste, combining thoroughly.

3 Divide the basil leaves between the cups, then put about 2 or 3 tablespoons of the fish mixture in each. Tap each cup gently to settle the contents. Place the cups on a rack in a steamer and steam over boiling water for 10–12 minutes.

4 Combine the remaining ¾ cup of coconut milk with the rice flour in a small pan and cook, stirring, over low heat until thick. Spread over the top of the fish pudding. Scatter a few shreds of lime leaf and chilli slices on top. Garnish with coriander leaves before serving.

# STEAMED FISH DUMPLINGS

*Khanom Jeeb Pla* (Makes about 20)

*One of the intriguing characteristics of Thai food is that so many things seem to be in miniature. Encased in a semi-transparent dough and steamed, the fish filling in these small dumplings is tasty but not hot. See colour plate on page 25.*

## FILLING
250 g (8 oz) white fish fillets
½ teaspoon crushed garlic
1 teaspoon finely grated fresh
    ginger
¼ teaspoon salt
⅛ teaspoon ground black
    pepper
1 teaspoon finely chopped
    coriander roots
1 teaspoon finely chopped
    kaffir lime rind
2 teaspoons fish sauce
2 tablespoons finely chopped
    spring onions

## DOUGH
1 cup (4 oz) gluten-free flour
    (e.g. wheat starch)
3 tablespoons cornflour
    (cornstarch)
¾ cup (6 fl oz) boiling water
1 tablespoon peanut oil
¼ teaspoon salt

1 **TO MAKE THE FILLING**, remove any traces of skin and bone from the fish and cut into pieces. Put through a food processor or chop very finely.

2 Add all the other filling ingredients and mix well. Cover and refrigerate while preparing the dough.

3 **TO MAKE THE DOUGH**, sift the flours into a bowl. In a small saucepan bring the water to the boil. Add the oil and salt and pour onto the flour, stirring constantly with a wooden spoon. When cool enough to handle, knead lightly until smooth.

4 Divide into two equal portions and shape each into a cylinder about 2.5 cm (1 in) in diameter. Wrap in plastic film to prevent the surface drying out.

5 Cut the dough into 1 cm (½ in) slices and roll out one slice at a time, until thin and about 10 cm (4 in) in diameter. Neaten the edges by cutting with a scone (biscuit) cutter.

6 Place a teaspoonful of the filling on the dough, fold over and press the edges together to seal. Make a decorative rope edge as described on page 13.

7 Place the dumplings on lightly oiled squares of greaseproof or non-stick baking paper in a steamer (or on a cake cooler placed on a trivet in a large pan). Cover the pan and steam over boiling water for 8–10 minutes. Serve warm with Sweet Dipping Sauce (*page 55*).

# SHALLOW-FRIED FISH CAKES

*Tod Mun Pla (Makes 6)*

*A characteristic of these fish cakes is their bouncy texture. Use a firm white fish such as ling or cod.*

300 g (10 oz) white fish fillets
2 teaspoons Red Curry Paste
   (*page 3*)
1 tablespoon fish sauce
2 tablespoons cornflour
   (cornstarch)
1 egg, beaten
1 teaspoon finely chopped red
   chilli, seeded
2 tablespoons chopped spring
   onions
½ cup finely sliced green
   beans
peanut oil for frying

1 Remove any trace of skin or bone from the fish fillets and cut into small pieces. Put into a food processor fitted with a steel blade and process until smooth.

2 Add the Red Curry Paste, fish sauce, cornflour and egg. Process again until well combined. With a spatula, scrape the fish paste into a bowl and stir in the red chilli, spring onions and beans.

3 Heat the oil in a frying pan to 1 cm (½ in) deep. With oiled hands form ¼ cup portions of the mixture into flat round cakes on an oiled frying spatula. Slide the fish cakes into the hot oil, a few at a time, and fry on medium heat until deep golden brown underneath. Turn the cakes over carefully and fry until the other side is done to the same golden brown colour. Remove with a slotted spoon and drain on absorbent paper. Serve warm or cold with Chilli and Cucumber Salad (*page 60*).

# MOULDED FISH CAKES

*Look Chin Pla* (Makes 12)

*The first time I encountered these was at a small, exclusive restaurant in Bangkok where palace cuisine was served. The tiny fish seemed to swim in their sea of green lettuce. The fragrance of lime rind, the pungency of garlic, chillies and pepper ensure these are no ordinary fish cakes.*

250 g (8 oz) white fish fillets
1 tablespoon Red Curry Paste
  (*page 3*)
2 tablespoons finely chopped
  spring onions
1 teaspoon finely chopped
  lime rind
½ teaspoon crushed garlic
2 teaspoons fish sauce
⅛ teaspoon ground black
  pepper
2 fresh red chillies, sliced
  (garnish)
spring onion tops (garnish)

---

NOTE *If you haven't any fish-shaped moulds, use scallop shells that can be bought very cheaply at fish markets. The shell shapes are pretty, though not quite as cute as the little fish.*

---

1 Remove any skin and bone from the fish and cut into pieces. Put through a mincer or chop very finely or grind in a food processor with all the other ingredients except the garnishes.

2 Oil 12 small moulds and press the fish mixture into them. Place in a steamer and steam over boiling water for 10 minutes, or until firm and opaque. Allow to cool slightly before turning out.

3 Decorate with slices of chilli and spring onion tops, and serve warm or cold.

A dainty selection of appetisers,
clockwise from top:
Water chestnut 'apples' (page 32),
Steamed fish dumplings (page 22),
Golden cups (page 12),
Deep-fried curry puffs (page 13).

*Prawn-filled omelette (page 29).*

# YOUNG CORN COBS WITH STEAMED FISH

*Pla Haw Kao Poad* (Serves 6)

*If fresh corn is available it needs no pre-cooking; the steaming will be sufficient. If using canned corn, drain well and pat dry on absorbent paper.*

1 × 455 g (14½ oz) can young
    corn cobs or 1 dozen fresh
    mini cobs
250 g (8 oz) white fish fillets
¼ teaspoon white pepper
2 teaspoons chopped garlic
1 tablespoon chopped
    coriander roots
1 teaspoon chopped galangal
    or ½ teaspoon ground
2 tablespoons finely sliced
    lemon grass or zest of
    1 lemon
1 tablespoon fish sauce
2 tablespoons finely chopped
    spring onions
2 teaspoons finely chopped
    red chillies, seeded

1 Drain the canned corn and blot dry on absorbent paper. If using fresh cobs, remove the husks and corn silk.

2 Remove any skin and bone from the fish and chop very finely, or put into a food processor with the pepper. Pound the garlic, coriander roots, galangal and lemon grass or zest to a paste, or reduce to a paste in a blender, adding the fish sauce to facilitate blending. Add to the fish with the spring onions and chillies and mix well.

3 Divide evenly into 12 portions and mould around the centre of each corn cob, firming on carefully and leaving both ends uncovered. Place in an oiled steamer and steam over boiling water for 8–10 minutes. Serve with a dipping sauce or salad.

# YOUNG CORN COBS WITH PRAWNS

*Goong Haw Hao Poad* (Makes about 12)

*A variation of Young Corn Cobs with Steamed Fish. Use a mixture of prawns and fish if prawns are unavailable.*

250 g (8 oz) raw prawn
  (shrimp) meat
1 egg white
1 tablespoon fish sauce
2 teaspoons Pepper and
  Coriander Paste (*page 8*)
4 tablespoons finely sliced
  spring onions or chopped
  shallots
1–2 teaspoons finely chopped
  red chillies, seeded
1 × 455 g (14½ oz) can young
  corn cobs or 1 dozen fresh
  mini cobs

1  Devein the prawns and place in a blender with the egg white, fish sauce, Pepper and Coriander Paste and half the spring onions. Reduce to a paste or chop the prawns finely and beat with a wooden spoon until paste-like. Mix in the remaining spring onions and the chillies so the prawn paste will be prettily flecked with colour.

2  With wet hands mould the mixture around the corn cobs, firming on carefully and leaving both ends uncovered. Place in an oiled steamer and steam over boiling water for 8–10 minutes, or until the prawn mixture changes colour. Serve with a dipping sauce or salad.

# PRAWN-FILLED OMELETTE

*Kai Yad Sai Goong* (Makes 10–12)

*See colour plate on page 26.*

250 g (8 oz) prawns (shrimp),
   shelled and deveined
2 teaspoons Pepper and
   Coriander Paste (*page 8*)
2 spring onions, sliced
2 tablespoons peanut oil
3 large eggs
2 tablespoons water
salt and white pepper
2 red chillies, shredded
fresh coriander (garnish)
strips of chilli (garnish)

1 Chop the prawns and mix with the Pepper and Coriander Paste and spring onions. Heat 1 tablespoon of the oil and stir-fry the prawns for 2 or 3 minutes. Turn onto a plate and set aside.

2 Beat the eggs lightly with the water, and add salt and pepper to taste. Heat an omelette pan, lightly grease it with some of the remaining oil and cook batches of 2 tablespoons of egg at a time to make small omelettes. Cook over low heat and do not let them brown. Turn, cooked side down, onto a plate. Repeat until all the mixture is used.

3 Place a tablespoon of the prawn mixture in the centre of each omelette and top with a few shreds of chilli and a coriander leaf. Fold in the ends of the omelette and roll up to enclose the filling. Garnish with chilli strips (dipped in hot water to make them pliable) and coriander sprigs. Serve with a dipping sauce if you like.

# CRACKER BALLS

*Pratad Lom* (Makes about 16)

*The name is a direct translation from the Thai, and these are little squares of bean-curd skin with a filling of savoury pork and prawn, gathered up and tied, steamed and then deep-fried.*

CHILLI SAUCE
½ cup (4 fl oz) white vinegar
3 red chillies, seeded and
    sliced
2 teaspoons finely chopped
    garlic
½ cup (4 oz) sugar
½ teaspoon salt
1 tablespoon fish sauce

250 g (8 oz) minced (ground)
    pork
125 g (4 oz) raw prawns
    (shrimp), deveined and
    chopped or 125 g (4 oz)
    flaked crab meat
½ teaspoon black peppercorns
1 teaspoon finely chopped
    garlic
½ teaspoon salt
4 tablespoons finely chopped
    fresh coriander including
    roots
¼ teaspoon finely grated
    kaffir lime rind
1 tablespoon fish sauce
1 egg, beaten
1 tablespoon cornflour
    (cornstarch)
half a sheet bean-curd skin
spring onion tops or garlic
    chives
peanut oil for frying

1 **TO MAKE THE CHILLI SAUCE**, place the vinegar, chillies and garlic in a blender and process at high speed. Pour into a saucepan, add the sugar and salt, and boil for 3–5 minutes. Add the fish sauce and allow to cool before using.

2 Put the pork and prawns or crab into a bowl.

3 Crush the peppercorns with a mortar and pestle, add the garlic, salt, coriander and lime rind, and pound to a paste. Mix into the pork and prawns together with the fish sauce, egg and cornflour until thoroughly combined.

4 Soak the bean-curd skin in warm water for a few minutes. Drain and cut into 10 cm (4 in) squares. Split the spring onion tops; if using chives, leave whole. Pour boiling water over them and leave for a minute until they become flexible. Drain on absorbent paper.

5 Place a tablespoon of the pork mixture in the centre of a square of bean-curd skin. Gather the top and tie with the spring onion (or chive) top. Continue until all the filling is used.

6 Steam over fast-boiling water for 10 minutes, remove from heat and cool. The cracker balls may be prepared ahead up to this point and refrigerated.

7 Shortly before serving, heat the oil in a wok and deep-fry a few balls at a time until golden brown and crisp. Drain on absorbent paper and serve warm with the Chilli Sauce.

# PRAWN ROLLS

*Hae Gun* (Makes about 12 slices)

*Dried bean-curd skin is used to wrap these tasty rolls.*

**2 large sheets dried bean-curd
    skin**
**250 g (8 oz) raw prawns
    (shrimp)**
**1 tablespoon cornflour
    (cornstarch)**
**2 tablespoons finely diced
    pork fat**
**½ teaspoon crushed garlic**
**½ teaspoon salt**
**½ teaspoon finely grated fresh
    ginger**
**¼ teaspoon ground black
    pepper**
**peanut oil for deep-frying**

1 Soak the bean-curd skin in warm water until soft, then drain.

2 Shell and devein the prawns and chop finely. Mix the prawns, cornflour, pork fat, garlic, salt, ginger and pepper thoroughly. Divide into two equal portions and shape each into a roll.

3 Place a roll on each sheet of bean-curd skin and roll up tightly. Put into a steamer over boiling water and steam for 10 minutes.

4 Allow to become cold, then deep-fry until brown. Cut into diagonal slices and serve with Sweet Dipping Sauce (*page 55*) or Chilli Sauce (*page 54*).

# WATER CHESTNUT 'APPLES'

*'Apple' Haeo* (Makes 20)

*Being invited to a party at Bangkok's famous Oriental Hotel is more than an extremely pleasurable experience, it is an education. Among the dainty appetisers offered to us were hollowed-out water chestnuts filled with tangy pomelo salad, the lids garnished with stems and leaves so they looked like bite-sized apples. These may be filled with other mixtures, such as the savoury filling in Pork-filled Sago Balls (page 16), or the chicken filling from Golden Cups (page 12). See colour plate on page 25.*

**20 water chestnuts**
**Pomelo Salad (*page 67*) or**
    **small quantity of other**
    **savoury filling**
**chilli or murraya leaves**
    **(garnish)**

**1** If fresh water chestnuts are available, peel and slice off the tops, then hollow out the centres with a small knife. Otherwise use canned chestnuts, selecting the largest and best shaped. Although flattened at the top and bottom, a more rounded effect is achieved if the tops are taken out in a slightly conical shape and inverted when being replaced. Hollow out the centre a little more to make room for the filling.

**2** Fill with Pomelo Salad or any of the savoury mixtures. A practical way is to save a little of the filling from any of the recipes. You will need only about a quarter of the quantity as the chestnuts don't hold very much. For this reason, emphasise the flavour of the filling. If using the Pomelo Salad, separate the fruit segments into small pieces, taking care not to crush them, and add more salt and chilli than if serving as a salad.

**3** With a wooden toothpick make a small hole in the conical side of the lid of each water chestnut for the decorative stem and leaves. Trim some chilli leaves, murraya or other non-toxic leaves to size with a pair of scissors and push into place.

# SOUPS

*I*n a Thai meal soups are not served as a first course as in Western meals. Instead, the bowl of soup comes with other dishes, to be sipped throughout the meal or spooned over rice to moisten it. These are generally light, clear soups.

On the other hand, there are soups which *are* the meal. Bowls laden with noodles of various kinds, and just a few slices of meat or some prawns.

Here is a selection of soups: some are gently seasoned and some will awaken your tastebuds with a jolt. A quantity of chilli, which blends and merges with other spices in a curry eaten with rice, can catch you by the throat when swallowed by the spoonful, so be wary. At the same time, don't allow yourself to be scared away from the tingling, refreshing flavours of such national favourites as Hot and Sour Prawn Soup, the famous *Tom Yum Goong* (page 39). There is also the mild and equally delicious Chicken with Galangal, a creamy coconut milk soup with the fragrance of fresh herbs.

# SOUP STOCK

1.5 litres (6 cups) water
1 large onion
1 large carrot
5 thin slices fresh ginger
5 coriander roots and attached
    stems
a few celery leaves (optional)
500 g (1 lb) chicken necks and
    backs or beef or pork bones
1 teaspoon salt
½ teaspoon whole black
    peppercorns

1  Bring the water to the boil while preparing the other ingredients.

2  Peel and quarter the onion and scrape the carrot. Put into the boiling water together with all the other ingredients. Return to the boil, then lower the heat, cover and simmer for 45 minutes to 1 hour, skimming any scum that rises to the surface. Strain and use right away, or cool and chill, removing any fat from the surface before freezing for future use.

# SOUP WITH CUCUMBER FLOWERS

*Tom Yum Tang Yud Sai* (Serves 6)

*Thai food has a delicate and beautiful look, even something as commonplace as a bowl of soup. Cucumber flowers are not difficult to make either.*

**SOUP**
1.5 litres (6 cups) Soup Stock
    (*page 34*)
2 kaffir lime leaves
1 tablespoon sugar
1 clove garlic, crushed
1 tablespoon fish sauce
2 tablespoons lime juice
1 teaspoon *Tom Yum* Paste
    (*page 6*)

**CUCUMBER FLOWERS**
2 small green cucumbers
125 g (4 oz) finely minced
    (ground) pork
2 teaspoons fish sauce
1 small clove garlic, crushed
⅛ teaspoon ground black
    pepper
1 strip kaffir lime rind, finely
    chopped

1  Put all the ingredients for the soup into a stainless steel or enamel pan and bring to a boil, covered, while preparing the cucumber flowers.

2  **TO MAKE THE CUCUMBER FLOWERS,** cut the cucumbers crosswise into short (3 cm/1½ in) lengths and with a sharp knife shape one end like the petals of a flower. Scoop out some of the seeds with a small spoon, leaving enough to form a base.

3  Combine the rest of the ingredients and mix well. Form into small balls and place one in each cucumber section.

4  Carefully place the flowers in the liquid, base downwards, and simmer gently for 8–10 minutes, just until the pork balls are cooked.

# SOUR SOUP WITH MEATBALLS

*Tom Yum Look Chin* (Serves 4)

*Refreshingly piquant but not too hot, this soup may be served on its own as a first course if you wish. See colour plate on page 44.*

1 tablespoon peanut oil

2 teaspoons Pepper and
  Coriander Paste (*page 8*)

1 teaspoon chopped garlic
  crushed with 2 teaspoons
  sugar

1.25 litres (5 cups) Soup Stock
  (*page 34*)

250 g (8 oz) Meatballs,
  prepared as on page 115
  but do not fry

2 dried kaffir lime leaves

½ cup spring onions, cut into
  short lengths

2 tablespoons fish sauce

90 g (3 oz) canned young corn
  cobs, drained

125 g (4 oz) rice noodles,
  soaked in hot water for
  10 minutes

1 chilli, seeded and finely
  sliced

1–2 tablespoons lime or lemon
  juice

1  Heat the oil and fry the Pepper and Coriander Paste until fragrant. Add the crushed garlic and sugar and stir in the stock. Bring to the boil, then drop in the meatballs. Add the lime leaves and simmer for 10 minutes.

2  Add all the remaining ingredients except the lime or lemon juice and simmer for 5 minutes longer. Add enough lime juice just before serving to give a slightly sour taste.

# HOT AND SOUR SEAFOOD SOUP

*Tom Yum Ta-Leh (Serves 4)*

*Depending on the strength of the chilli used in the soup, this can be more than slightly pungent. Some chillies are hotter than others, and as a general rule the smaller the chilli, the hotter it is. Serve this with steamed jasmine rice.*

125 g (4 oz) fresh raw prawns
   (shrimp)
1 tablespoon peanut oil
1 teaspoon dried shrimp paste
1 tablespoon Pepper and
   Coriander Paste (*page 8*)
4 dried or frozen kaffir lime
   leaves
1 red chilli, split and seeded
2 stalks lemon grass, very
   thinly sliced diagonally
1.5 litres (6 cups) fish or
   prawn stock
1 cup shredded cabbage or
   sliced beans
125 g (4 oz) fish fillets
2 spring onions, sliced into
   2.5 cm (1 in) lengths
1 tablespoon lime or lemon
   juice
1 tablespoon fish sauce
2 teaspoons palm sugar
red chilli, sliced (garnish)

1 Shell the prawns, reserving the heads and shells. Devein the prawns, rinse quickly and dry on absorbent paper. Heat the oil and fry the prawn heads and shells until pink.

2 Add the shrimp paste and Pepper and Coriander Paste, and stir-fry for 1 minute. Add the kaffir lime leaves, chilli, lemon grass and stock, and simmer for 15 minutes.

3 Strain and return the liquid to the saucepan with the cabbage or beans. Simmer 10 minutes longer.

4 Add the fish and prawns and simmer a further 4 or 5 minutes, until the fish turns white and opaque, and the prawns pink. Stir in the spring onions, lime or lemon juice, fish sauce and palm sugar. Serve in bowls, garnished with slices of red chilli.

# SOUR AND SPICY CHICKEN SOUP

*Tom Yum Gai (Serves 6)*

*The name says it all – so temper the spiciness with steamed rice.*

6 chicken drumsticks, skin
   removed
1 teaspoon chopped garlic
3 or 4 red chillies, seeded and
   sliced
1 tablespoon Pepper and
   Coriander Paste (*page 8*)
1.5 litres (6 cups) chicken
   Soup Stock (*page 34*)
2 fresh, frozen or dried kaffir
   lime leaves
¾ cup chopped onions or
   shallots
3 slices fresh or bottled
   galangal
2 stems lemon grass, finely
   sliced
2 teaspoons sugar
2 tablespoons fish sauce
2 tablespoons lime juice,
   strained
chopped fresh coriander
   (garnish)
sliced chillies (optional)

---

**NOTE** *If you have some* Tom Yum
Paste (page 6) *in the refrigerator or
freezer, use a tablespoon of paste to
marinate the chicken, and continue as
in the recipe.*

---

1 Chop each drumstick in half.

2 Pound the garlic, chillies and Pepper and Coriander
Paste together, and mix with the chicken pieces. Allow to
marinate for 15 minutes.

3 Place the stock, lime leaves, onions, galangal, lemon
grass and sugar in a large saucepan, add the chicken and
simmer for 30 minutes, or until the chicken is very tender.

4 Add the fish sauce and lime juice. Check the flavour,
which should be spicy and sour. Serve with coriander
leaves sprinkled over, and extra sliced chillies if you like it
really hot.

# HOT AND SOUR PRAWN SOUP

*Tom Yum Goong (Serves 6)*

*This is the best known Thai soup, and one that really wakes up the tastebuds. Lots of lime juice and chillies are essential, as are other fresh herbs such as lemon grass and lime leaves.*

500 g (1 lb) medium-sized raw
　　prawns (shrimp)
1 tablespoon peanut oil
2 litres (8 cups) water
1 teaspoon salt
2 stems fresh lemon grass,
　　thinly sliced or 4 strips
　　lemon zest
4 fresh, frozen or dried kaffir
　　lime leaves
4 slices galangal, fresh or
　　bottled
2 or 3 fresh chillies, seeded
2 teaspoons chopped garlic
1–2 tablespoons fish sauce
3 tablespoons lime juice
1 fresh red chilli, seeded and
　　sliced (garnish)
2 tablespoons chopped
　　coriander leaves (garnish)
4 spring onions with green
　　tops, chopped (garnish)

---

**NOTE** *Instead of having to scramble around for the ingredients each time, make a batch of* Tom Yum *paste (page 6), which lasts for months in the refrigerator, whenever you have them all to hand. Then a bowl of this tangy soup will take only as long as boiling the water! Just stir 3 tablespoons* Tom Yum *paste into 1.25–1.5 litres (5–6 cups) boiling stock or water, drop in the prawns and simmer only until they turn pink. Garnish with coriander leaves and serve.*

---

**1** Shell and devein the prawns, save the heads and shells and dry them on absorbent paper. Heat the oil in a saucepan and fry the heads and shells until they turn red.

**2** Add the water, salt, lemon grass or lemon rind, lime leaves, galangal, chillies and garlic. Bring to the boil, cover and simmer for 20 minutes. Strain the stock.

**3** Return the stock to the saucepan and add the prawns, then simmer for 3–4 minutes or until the prawns are cooked. Add the fish sauce and lime juice to taste, and remove from the heat at once. Serve in a tureen or in soup plates, sprinkled with the chilli, coriander and spring onions.

# MUSHROOM *TOM YUM*

## *Tom Yum Hed* (Serves 6)

*Mushrooms are very much part of the Thai diet, and straw mushrooms, in particular, are plentiful in Thailand. Fresh straw mushrooms, golden mushrooms and oyster mushrooms are grown commercially in Australia. Fresh straw mushrooms should always be blanched as follows and may then be stored in the refrigerator for up to a week.*

250 g (8 oz) fresh straw or
    button mushrooms
1.5 litres (6 cups) water
1 teaspoon salt
2 stems fresh lemon grass,
    thinly sliced or 4 strips
    lemon zest
4 fresh, frozen or dried kaffir
    lime leaves
4 slices galangal, fresh or
    bottled
2 or 3 fresh chillies
2 teaspoons chopped garlic
1 cup (8 fl oz) thick coconut
    milk
1–2 tablespoons fish sauce
3 tablespoons lime juice
1 fresh red chilli, seeded and
    sliced (garnish)
2 tablespoons chopped
    coriander leaves (garnish)
4 spring onions, including
    green tops, chopped
    (garnish)

1 Wipe the mushrooms, and if using straw mushrooms, bring a pan of lightly salted water to the boil and simmer them for 3 minutes.

2 Put the water, salt, lemon grass, lime leaves, galangal, chillies and garlic into a saucepan. Bring to the boil, cover and simmer for 20 minutes.

3 Add the mushrooms and simmer for a further 5 minutes.

4 Stir in the coconut milk. Add the fish sauce and the lime juice to taste, then remove from the heat at once. Serve in a tureen or in soup plates, sprinkled with chilli, coriander and spring onions.

# PRAWN SOUP WITH MUSHROOMS

*Kaeng Chud Goong Hed (Serves 6)*

*A mild soup in which the flavours are those of prawns, dried shiitake mushrooms and garlic.*

60 g (2 oz) bean starch
  noodles
24 dried lily buds
6 dried shiitake mushrooms
2 teaspoons finely chopped
  garlic
½ cup chopped fresh
  coriander, including roots
375 g (12 oz) raw prawns
  (shrimp)
3 tablespoons peanut oil
1.5 litres (6 cups) water
1 medium onion, finely sliced
4 spring onions, finely sliced
2 tablespoons fish sauce
1 teaspoon sugar
fresh coriander leaves
  (garnish)

1 Put the noodles in a bowl and pour boiling water over them to cover. Leave to soak. In another bowl soak the lily buds and the mushrooms in hot water for 30 minutes. Drain.

2 Pinch off the hard ends of the lily buds and tie a knot in the middle of each one. Cut off the tough stems of the mushrooms and slice the caps thinly. Cut the noodles into short lengths.

3 Pound the garlic and coriander together, or put into an electric blender with a little water and purée.

4 Shell and devein the prawns, and use the heads and shells to make a stock. To do this, first fry them in a tablespoon of the oil in a large saucepan, then add the water and simmer for 20 minutes. Strain the stock before using.

5 Heat the remaining oil and fry the onion until soft and translucent, stirring now and then. Add the garlic and coriander purée and fry, stirring constantly, over medium heat until fragrant. Add the prawns and fry until they change colour, then pour in the hot stock, lily buds, mushroom slices and noodles.

6 Bring the soup to the boil, simmer gently for 5 minutes, then stir in the spring onions, fish sauce and sugar. Taste and adjust the seasoning. Serve garnished with fresh coriander leaves.

# MILD SOUP WITH STUFFED MUSHROOMS

*Kaeng Chud Hed Yud Sai* (Serves 6)

*If you are timid about hot flavours, this is a good dish to try!*

12 medium-sized dried
   shiitake mushrooms
125 g (4 oz) minced (ground)
   pork or chopped raw
   prawns (shrimp)
1 teaspoon finely chopped
   garlic
3 spring onions, finely
   chopped
1 tablespoon finely chopped
   coriander
1 tablespoon Golden
   Mountain Sauce (*page 209*)
¼ teaspoon ground black
   pepper
1 tablespoon finely chopped
   water chestnuts
1.5 litres (6 cups) chicken
   Soup Stock (*page 34*),
   strained
half a green cucumber
1 tablespoon fish sauce or to
   taste
chilli slices (optional)

1 Pour boiling water over the mushrooms in a bowl and leave to soak for 30 minutes. Squeeze out any excess water and cut off the stems – these may be simmered in the stock for extra flavour but should be removed before serving.

2 Combine the pork or prawns (or a mixture of both) with the garlic, 2 tablespoons of the chopped spring onions, coriander, Golden Mountain sauce, pepper and water chestnuts. Mix well.

3 Pack the mixture into the drained mushroom caps and cook for 15 to 20 minutes in 3 cups (24 fl oz) of the chicken stock. (If dropped into deep stock the mushrooms will tumble over, causing the filling to fall out, but this won't happen once the filling is cooked.)

4 Peel the cucumber and cut in half lengthwise, remove the seeds and slice crosswise.

5 Add the remaining stock, cucumber and fish sauce to the pan and simmer for 3 or 4 minutes.

6 To serve, place 2 mushrooms in each soup plate. Ladle the soup over and garnish with the remaining spring onions and some chilli slices, if you like.

*Chicken and galangal in coconut milk (page 49),*
*Mixed vegetable soup (page 45).*

*Sour soup with meatballs (page 36).*

# MIXED VEGETABLE SOUP

*Kaeng Liang Pak* (Serves 6)

*A mild, clear vegetable soup flavoured with shrimp. See colour plate on page 43.*

⅓ cup dried shrimp

5 coriander roots

2 teaspoons chopped garlic

1 teaspoon dried shrimp paste,
   roasted

¾ cup chopped onions

1.25 litres (5 cups) Soup Stock
   (*page 34*)

4 cups prepared vegetables
   such as bamboo shoots,
   beans, straw mushrooms,
   young corn cobs, zucchini
   (courgettes)

2 tablespoons fish sauce

1 teaspoon palm sugar

½ cup sweet basil or coriander
   leaves

---

NOTE *If you have Pepper and
Coriander Paste* (page 8) *to hand,
2 teaspoons may be substituted for the
coriander roots and garlic; the soup
will be a darker colour.*

---

1  Soak the dried shrimp in hot water for 10 minutes. Put into a blender or food processor with the coriander roots, garlic, shrimp paste and onions. Add a little water if necessary and purée.

2  Add the paste to the stock and bring to the boil. Add the vegetables to the stock, putting in those that require longer cooking first and the quick-cooking ones last. Stir in the fish sauce and palm sugar, and throw in the basil or coriander leaves just before serving. Serve hot.

# PUMPKIN AND COCONUT SOUP

*Gaeng Liang Fak Thong* (Serves 6)

*A rich, delightfully flavoured soup. If 'pumpkin soup' conjures up a taste-memory of Western-style pumpkin soup, you are in for a surprise!*

500 g (1 lb) ripe pumpkin, peeled and cubed
1 tablespoon lime or lemon juice
2 teaspoons dried tamarind pulp
½ cup (4 fl oz) hot water
½ cup dried shrimp
½ cup chopped onions or shallots
3 or 4 red chillies, seeded and chopped
1 stalk lemon grass, finely chopped or zest of 1 lemon
1 teaspoon dried shrimp paste
2 cups (16 fl oz) thin coconut milk
1 cup (8 fl oz) thick coconut milk
½ cup basil leaves
1 tablespoon fish sauce
1 cup (8 fl oz) chicken stock or water (optional)

1 Place the pumpkin in a bowl and sprinkle with the lime juice.

2 Soak the dried tamarind in the hot water for 10 minutes, squeeze to dissolve the pulp and strain through a nylon sieve. Set aside.

3 Soak the dried shrimp in some hot water for 10 minutes, then drain. Pound together with the onions, chillies, lemon grass or zest and shrimp paste; or place these ingredients in a food processor or blender and reduce to a paste.

4 Put the paste into a saucepan with the thin coconut milk and stir until boiling. Simmer for 5 minutes then stir in the tamarind liquid and pumpkin. Stir again and simmer for another 10 minutes, or until the pumpkin is tender.

5 Stir in the thick coconut milk and basil leaves, and bring back to the boil, adding fish sauce to taste. If necessary thin the soup with a little chicken stock or water.

**NOTE** *Ripe pumpkin is brightly coloured, firm textured and sweet in flavour. An unripe pumpkin has none of these desirable characteristics. It is better to buy it in the piece so you can judge the colour – even experts can't tell how ripe it is until it is cut.*

# CHICKEN AND NOODLE SOUP

*Sen Mee Gai (Serves 6)*

*Nothing like its namesake that comes out of a packet, this soup has real slices of chicken and the tang of fresh herbs.*

1.5 litres (6 cups) chicken Soup Stock (*page 34*)
1 whole chicken breast
2 teaspoons Pepper and Coriander Paste (*page 8*)
2 teaspoons fish sauce
1 cup fresh bean sprouts, trimmed
½ cup sliced spring onions
125 g (4 oz) rice vermicelli, soaked for 10 minutes in hot water
1 or 2 sliced red or green chillies (garnish)
coriander leaves (garnish)

1  Make the stock, and when it is almost ready slide the chicken breast into the pan and simmer very gently for 6–8 minutes. Turn off the heat and let the chicken remain in the liquid until quite cool. Lift out, and remove any skin and bones, and cut the meat into neat slices.

2  Reheat the stock and stir in the Pepper and Coriander Paste, fish sauce, bean sprouts and spring onions. Add the drained rice vermicelli and heat through. Stir in the chicken slices and serve garnished with chilli slices and coriander leaves.

# CHICKEN AND VEGETABLE SOUP

*Kaeng Chud Gai Pak* (Serves 6)

*A satisfying soup, and if the chillies are omitted it is quite mild in flavour.*

1 cup (8 fl oz) hot water
6 dried shiitake mushrooms
75 g (2½ oz) bean starch
   noodles
2 coriander roots or 6 stalks,
   chopped
2 teaspoons chopped garlic
3 red or yellow chillies, seeded
   and sliced
¼ cup spring onions, chopped
250 g (8 oz) chicken breast
   fillet, sliced
1 litre (4 cups) chicken stock
¼ cup spring onions, cut into
   4 cm (1½ in) lengths
1 cup young corn cobs, cut
   into bite-sized pieces
½ cup sliced water chestnuts
½ cup finely sliced bamboo
   shoots
fresh coriander leaves
   (garnish)

1 Pour the water over the mushrooms in a bowl and leave to soak for 30 minutes. Drain, reserving the soaking water. Discard the stems and slice the caps.

2 Soak the noodles in hot water for 15 minutes, drain and cut into short lengths.

3 Pound the coriander roots, garlic, chillies and spring onions to a paste and mix with the chicken. Leave to marinate for 10 minutes.

4 Heat the stock, add the mushrooms and simmer for 5 minutes. Add the next 4 ingredients and simmer for a further 5 minutes. Garnish with coriander leaves before serving.

# CHICKEN AND GALANGAL IN COCONUT MILK

*Tom Kha Gai* (Serves 6)

*A distinctive soup which is probably one of the two most popular in Thai cuisine. The other is* Tom Yum Goong, *Hot and Sour Prawn Soup (page 39). This, by contrast, is creamy rich with coconut milk, and the predominant flavour is that of the aromatic rhizome, galangal. See colour plate on page 43.*

6 slices fresh, bottled or dried
   galangal
1 small roasting chicken, cut
   into bite-sized pieces
3 cups (24 fl oz) thin coconut
   milk
¼ teaspoon black pepper
3 fresh coriander roots,
   crushed
2 stems lemon grass, thinly
   sliced or zest of 1 lemon
3 fresh green chillies
1½ teaspoons salt
3 or 4 fresh or frozen kaffir
   lime leaves
1 cup (8 fl oz) thick coconut
   milk
1 tablespoon fish sauce
lime juice to taste
3 tablespoons chopped fresh
   coriander leaves

1 If using dried galangal, soak it in hot water to cover for 30 minutes.

2 Put the chicken into a saucepan with the thin coconut milk, galangal, pepper, coriander roots, lemon grass or lemon, chillies, salt and lime leaves.

3 Bring to the boil over low heat. Simmer, uncovered, until the chicken is tender, stirring occasionally. Add the thick coconut milk and stir constantly until it returns to the boil. Remove from the heat and stir in the fish sauce and lime juice. Serve sprinkled with chopped coriander leaves and accompanied with steamed jasmine rice.

# PORK AND MUSHROOM SOUP

*Kaeng Chud Moo Hed* (*Serves 6*)

*This delicious soup is not too hot, and for an even milder flavour, skip the chillies.*

6 dried shiitake mushrooms
1 tablespoon peanut oil
1 tablespoon Pepper and
    Coriander Paste (*page 8*)
125 g (4 oz) lean pork, diced
1.25 litres (5 cups) chicken or
    pork Soup Stock (*page 34*)
2 kaffir lime leaves
2 chillies, sliced (optional)
125 g (4 oz) raw prawns
    (shrimp), shelled and
    deveined
1–2 tablespoons fish sauce
1 teaspoon palm sugar
coriander leaves (garnish)

1  Soak the mushrooms in hot water for 30 minutes to soften. Remove the stems and discard.

2  Heat the oil and fry the Pepper and Coriander Paste, add the diced pork and stir-fry until the colour changes. Add the stock and lime leaves and simmer for 25 minutes, until the pork is tender.

3  Add the mushrooms and chillies, if using, and cook for 10 minutes, then add the prawns and cook for 3 minutes more. Flavour with the fish sauce and palm sugar, and garnish with coriander leaves before serving.

# BEEF SOUP WITH COCONUT MILK

*Tom Kha Nuer* (Serves 6)

*This soup remains spicy enough to spoon over rice, even though its 'bite' is tempered by coconut milk and palm sugar.*

375 g (12 oz) lean rump or
   round steak
2 teaspoons Pepper and
   Coriander Paste (*page 8*)
½ teaspoon grated kaffir or
   Tahitian lime zest
1 litre (4 cups) thin coconut
   milk
2 stems lemon grass, very
   thinly sliced or zest of 1
   lemon
5 slices fresh or bottled
   galangal, thinly sliced
3 frozen or dried kaffir lime
   leaves
1 cup (8 fl oz) thick coconut
   milk
½ cup spring onions, sliced
2 or 3 sliced chillies, seeded
2 teaspoons palm sugar
1–2 tablespoons fish sauce
4 tablespoons chopped fresh
   coriander

NOTE *For a lighter soup, replace part of the coconut milk with water or a light stock.*

1 Trim any fat or sinew from the beef and cut into very thin strips.

2 Combine the Pepper and Coriander Paste, lime zest and beef strips, mix well and leave to marinate for 10–15 minutes.

3 Bring the thin coconut milk to the boil, stirring constantly. Add the beef, lemon grass, galangal and lime leaves and stir until it returns to the boil.

4 Reduce the heat and simmer, uncovered, for 30 minutes or until the meat is tender. Stir in the thick coconut milk, spring onions, chillies, palm sugar and fish sauce. Top with fresh coriander.

# COMBINATION SOUP

*Kaeng Chud Ruam Mit* (*Serves 4–6*)

*The different tastes of pork, chicken, prawns and vegetables give this soup a variety of textures and flavours. If you prefer it mild, omit the sliced chilli.*

3 dried shiitake mushrooms
90 g (3 oz) pork
90 g (3 oz) chicken breast
    fillet
90 g (3 oz) raw prawns
    (shrimp)
60 g (2 oz) bean starch
    noodles
1 tablespoon chopped fresh
    coriander
½ teaspoon black peppercorns
1 teaspoon finely chopped
    garlic
1 tablespoon peanut oil
1.5 litres (6 cups) Soup Stock
    (*page 34*) or prawn stock
1 tablespoon Golden
    Mountain Sauce (*page 209*)
1 tablespoon fish sauce
6 spring onions, sliced
1 small green cucumber,
    peeled, seeded and sliced
1 egg, very lightly beaten
sliced chilli, chopped fresh
    coriander or spring onion
    tops (garnish)

1  Soak the dried mushrooms in hot water for 30 minutes. Squeeze out any excess moisture, discard the stems and slice the caps.

2  Slice the pork and chicken into thin strips. Devein the prawns and cut in half if large. Soak the bean starch noodles in hot water for 10–15 minutes, drain and cut into short (2.5 cm/1 in) lengths.

3  Pound the coriander, peppercorns and garlic together, or use 2 teaspoons Pepper and Coriander Paste (*page 8*). Heat the oil and fry the pounded mixture, stirring, until fragrant.

4  Add the pork and chicken and stir-fry until they change colour. Add the stock, Golden Mountain sauce, fish sauce, mushrooms and noodles, and simmer for 15 minutes.

5  Stir in the spring onions, cucumber and prawns, and cook for 3 or 4 minutes. Slowly dribble in the egg, stirring lightly as it sets. Sprinkle with sliced chilli, chopped coriander or spring onion tops before serving.

# SALADS, SAUCES AND DIPS

*A* Thai salad can be cool, refreshing and pungent all at once. On my trips to Thailand I've been fascinated by the numerous leaves, roots and shoots that are eaten raw, dipped in one or another of the hot sauces. Thais are very keen on raw vegetables and include them in the daily diet both for their food value and taste.

Alongside the vegetables will be the essential Thai dipping sauce, *nam prik*. There is not just one, but many variations of this. The word *nam* means water, and *prik* means chilli, so it doesn't take much imagination to know it will be rather hot. In most mixtures, however, there is enough palm sugar to take the edge off the spicy chilli and make the sauce a pleasantly stimulating experience.

# CHILLI SAUCE

*Saus Prik* *(Makes about ¾ cup)*

6–8 large dried chillies
½ cup (4 fl oz) white vinegar
3 fresh red chillies, seeded and
   sliced
2 teaspoons finely chopped
   garlic
½ cup (4 oz) sugar
½ teaspoon salt
1 tablespoon fish sauce

1 Remove the stems and seeds from the dried chillies, break the chillies in pieces and soak in hot water for 10 minutes. Drain.

2 Place the vinegar, both the dried and fresh chillies, and the garlic in a blender and blend at high speed, then pour into a saucepan. Add the sugar and salt and boil for 10 minutes, then add the fish sauce and allow to cool.

# SWEET CHILLI SAUCE

*Saus Prik Wan* *(Makes about 2 cups/16 fl oz)*

*While this sauce is sweet, it is also hot. Much depends on the variety of chillies used – small chillies are very much hotter than the larger kind. This sauce seems to keep almost indefinitely.*

125 g (4 oz) fresh red chillies
125 g (4 oz) sultanas
4 cloves garlic, peeled
2 teaspoons chopped fresh
   ginger
¾ cup (6 fl oz) white vinegar
¾ cup (6 fl oz) water
1½ cups (12 oz) white sugar
2 teaspoons salt

1 Wash the chillies and snip off the stalks. If you don't wish to include the seeds with their extra heat, slit and seed the chillies and put them into an electric blender or food processor with the sultanas, garlic, ginger and enough vinegar to purée the mixture.

2 Pour into an enamel or stainless steel saucepan and add the rest of the ingredients. Bring to the boil and simmer, stirring occasionally, until the sauce has thickened slightly. Cool, then pour into sterilised bottles and seal.

# SWEET DIPPING SAUCE

*Saus Wan* *(Makes about ¾ cup/6 fl oz)*

4 tablespoons sugar
½ cup (4 fl oz) cold water
2 tablespoons fish sauce
red and green chillies, seeded
    and finely sliced
1 tablespoon lime juice or
    vinegar

Stir the sugar with the cold water until the sugar dissolves, then add the remaining ingredients. This gives a very clear, glossy sauce.

# *NAM PRIK* PHUKET

*(Serves 4)*

*In a small coffee shop in Phuket I had some robustly flavoured and satisfying peasant-style food. The lady who owned and ran the shop was pleased by my interest and demonstrated this particularly delicious dipping sauce. Serve with raw or lightly cooked vegetables.*

½ cup dried shrimp
2 large cloves garlic, roughly
    chopped
3 purple shallots or 1 small
    brown onion, roughly
    chopped
5 fresh hot chillies, sliced
2 teaspoons shrimp paste
1 tablespoon sugar
1 tablespoon palm sugar
2 tablespoons lime juice
1 tablespoon fish sauce

**1** Soak the dried shrimp in warm water for 10 minutes. Drain well. Preheat a griller (broiler).

**2** Put the garlic, shallots or onion and chillies into a mortar and pestle and pound to a paste.

**3** Wrap the shrimp paste in foil, making a flat parcel, and place under the preheated griller (broiler) for 5 minutes on each side.

**4** Add the grilled shrimp paste to the mortar and pound again, then add the sugar, palm sugar, lime juice and fish sauce. Add a little water to make a dipping consistency.

# PEANUT SAUCE

*Nam Jim Tua* (Makes about 2 cups/16 fl oz)

*Use about 1 cup of this sauce for the Stuffed Chicken Wings (page 84) and store the rest in the refrigerator ready to serve on vegetables or with grilled meats like satays.*

1 tablespoon peanut oil
2–3 teaspoons crushed chilli
  flakes
½ cup finely sliced shallots
1 tablespoon Red Curry Paste
  (*page 3*)
2 kaffir lime leaves, finely
  shredded
1–1½ cups (8–12 fl oz)
  coconut milk
¾ cup crunchy peanut butter
2 tablespoons palm sugar
2 tablespoons tamarind liquid
2–3 tablespoons lime juice

1  Heat the oil and carefully fry the chilli flakes on low heat. Add the shallots, Red Curry Paste and lime leaves and cook until fragrant.

2  Stir in 1 cup (8 fl oz) of the coconut milk, the peanut butter, palm sugar and tamarind liquid. Bring to the boil, stirring, and add the lime juice. Thin to a pouring consistency with the remaining coconut milk or water.

# PORK AND PEANUT DIP

*Moo Lon* (Makes about 1½ cups/12 fl oz)

*This dip is primarily for the Deep-fried Rice Crackers (page 172) but is also nice with raw or lightly cooked crisp vegetables.*

¾ cup (6 fl oz) coconut milk
1 teaspoon Pepper and
  Coriander Paste (*page 8*)
125 g (4 oz) minced (ground)
  pork
2 tablespoons peanut butter
2 spring onions, finely sliced
2 tablespoons fish sauce
1 teaspoon palm sugar
1 red chilli, seeded and finely
  sliced

1  Heat the coconut milk until bubbling and cook the Pepper and Coriander Paste until fragrant.

2  Add the pork and fry, stirring constantly, until it changes colour. Stir in the peanut butter, spring onions, fish sauce, palm sugar and chilli.

3  Turn the heat down and simmer for 10 minutes or until the pork is tender. If necessary, add a little water to the sauce to produce a dipping consistency.

# EGGPLANT DIPPING SAUCE

*Nam Prik Makua* *(Serves 6)*

*This is an ideal dipping sauce to serve with a platter of raw or lightly cooked vegetables, which is part of every Thai meal.*

**1 medium-sized eggplant (aubergine), about 300 g (10 oz), peeled and diced**
**1 lime**
**2 small purple shallots, sliced or 2 tablespoons chopped spring onions**
**¼ teaspoon crushed garlic**
**½ teaspoon salt or to taste**
**1 teaspoon palm sugar**
**1 or 2 fresh red chillies, seeded and sliced**

1 Have ready a stainless steel saucepan with lightly salted boiling water. Drop the eggplant into the boiling water, cover and cook for about 8 minutes or until tender. Drain.

2 Finely grate the lime rind and squeeze the juice. Put the eggplant into the container of an electric blender with the lime rind and juice, shallots or spring onions, garlic, salt, sugar and chillies.

3 Blend at high speed to combine all the ingredients. Taste, and add salt or lime juice if necessary. Serve in a small bowl with vegetables for dipping.

# SHRIMP DIP WITH TAMARIND

*Nam Prik Pao* *(Makes about 2 cups/16 fl oz)*

*Serve as a dip with Deep-fried Rice Crackers (page 172), raw or lightly cooked vegetables, or as an accompaniment with rice and curries. Keeps for weeks in a glass jar in the refrigerator.*

1 cup dried shrimp
10 medium-sized dried
    chillies, seeded and soaked
1 cup chopped onion
1–2 tablespoons chopped
    garlic
½ cup (4 fl oz) peanut oil
½ cup palm sugar
1–2 teaspoons tamarind pulp
    concentrate (*page 212*)
¼ cup (2 fl oz) water
2 tablespoons fish sauce
2 teaspoons lime juice

1  Put the dried shrimp in an electric blender and blend on high speed until reduced to a floss. Empty into a bowl and without washing the blender put in the drained chillies, onion, garlic and the peanut oil, and blend on high speed until puréed.

2  Pour into a shallow pan and fry on medium heat, stirring constantly, until the oil comes to the surface.

3  Add the palm sugar, tamarind, water and shrimp floss and simmer a further 5 minutes, or until a thick dipping consistency. Add the fish sauce and simmer for 2–3 minutes. Remove from the heat and when cool, stir in the lime juice.

# FRESH SALAD WITH *NAM PRIK*

*Pak Nam Prik (Serves 4)*

Nam prik *is the term applied to various dipping sauces based on fish sauce and chilli. Other ingredients may vary, but these two are always present. The mixture may be cooked or simply mixed together. The most useful implement in making a* nam prik *is a primitive mortar and pestle. While electric blenders will combine a* nam prik *and the flavour may be correct, the consistency is altered and is usually too liquid. It should be thick enough to coat the raw or lightly blanched vegetable dipped into it. This dish makes an ideal appetiser.*

3 tablespoons dried shrimp
1 clove garlic, chopped
2 shallots or small red onions, chopped
2 fresh red chillies, chopped
2 tablespoons lime juice
2 teaspoons palm sugar
2 tablespoons fish sauce
2 tablespoons water
1 bunch young green asparagus
a handful tender stringless beans
2 medium-sized carrots, sliced
4 white cabbage leaves, cut into eighths
2 or 3 spring onions, sliced into 2.5 cm (1 in) lengths
a few red radishes
2 green cucumbers

NOTE *Look for dried shrimp that are a bright salmon pink colour and fairly soft when pressed through the packet. This indicates they are fresh. Those which are very hard and are a dull colour have been around for much longer and, while they may be used, are not as desirable.*

1 Wash the dried shrimp and put in a shallow dish. Pour over enough hot water to cover. Leave them to soak for about 10 minutes. Put the drained shrimp into a mortar and pestle with the garlic, onions and chillies, and pound to a paste. Gradually stir in the lime juice, palm sugar, fish sauce and water.

2 Wash the asparagus thoroughly, snap off any tough ends, and peel the bottom half of each spear to ensure it will be tender and edible from tip to base. Blanch in a pan of boiling water for 3 or 4 minutes only – they should still have some snap to them. Plunge into a bowl of ice water to set the colour and stop the cooking. When cold, drain. Prepare the beans in the same way.

3 Peel the carrots and with a sharp knife make small V-shaped cuts at regular intervals down the length of each carrot. Slice. Cut the cabbage into small round shapes.

4 Slit the ends of the spring onions with a strong pin. Drop into ice water for a few minutes for the ends to curl. Use a thin-bladed knife to make cuts at regular intervals around the radishes. Drop them into iced water for the 'petals' to open.

6 Cut the ends off the cucumbers, then cut into tulip shapes with a sharp, pointed knife. Make leaves with the rest of the cucumbers, some with the skin on and others peeled. With a knife, cut oblong slices, avoiding the seeds in the centre. Shape, and use the point of the knife for leaf markings. Arrange all vegetables on a plate, cover with plastic film and refrigerate until ready to serve.

7 Serve the sauce in a small bowl with the vegetables.

# CHILLI AND CUCUMBER SALAD

*Nam Jim Tang Guar* (*Makes about ⅔ cup*)

*A small, relish-type salad to accompany any appetiser.*

2 tablespoons sugar
2 tablespoons water
2 tablespoons fish sauce
2 tablespoons lime juice
½ cup finely sliced cucumber
2 tablespoons sliced purple
   shallots
1 red chilli, seeded and sliced

Stir in the sugar with the water until dissolved, then add the fish sauce and lime juice. Add the cucumber, shallots and chilli.

*Seafood salad (page 76).*

*Mango salad (page 63).*

# MANGO SALAD

*Yum Ma Muang (Serves 4)*

*If you have access to unripe or half-ripe mangoes, this is a seasonal treat. You can, however, enjoy this refreshing salad all year round by substituting tart cooking apples. See colour plate on page 62.*

2 firm mangoes or green
    apples
½ teaspoon salt
1 tablespoon peanut oil
2 teaspoons dried garlic flakes
4 spring onions, thinly sliced
125 g (4 oz) pork fillet
    (tenderloin), finely chopped
1 tablespoon dried shrimp,
    reduced to a floss in an
    electric blender
1 tablespoon fish sauce
1 tablespoon lime juice
1 teaspoon palm sugar
2 tablespoons crushed, roasted
    peanuts (garnish)
1 or 2 red chillies, finely
    seeded and sliced (garnish)

1 Peel the fruit and slice thinly, cut the slices into julienne and put into a large bowl. If using apples, add the lime juice now to prevent discolouring. Sprinkle with salt and toss gently.

2 Heat the oil and fry the garlic until pale golden. Lift out and drain. In the same oil fry the spring onions and set aside.

3 Quickly fry the pork until cooked and brown, add the shrimp floss, fish sauce, lime juice (if using mangoes), and palm sugar.

4 Just before serving put everything together in a bowl, toss lightly and garnish with the peanuts and chillies.

# GREEN PAWPAW SALAD

*Som Tam* (Serves 4)

*Now readily available where fresh Asian ingredients are sold, the green pawpaw or papaya used in this salad is not slightly under-ripe, it is very green indeed, and the flesh is quite white. It is very popular in Thailand, where some stalls are devoted solely to this salad. Each order is freshly made, the ingredients combined and lightly pounded in a mortar and pestle.*

2 cups finely shredded green
    pawpaw (papaya)
½ cup young green beans,
    sliced (use snake beans if
    available)
2 tablespoons dried shrimp
2 tablespoons crushed, roasted
    peanuts

DRESSING
1 small clove garlic
2 purple shallots or 1 small
    brown onion
2 fresh chillies, seeded
2 teaspoons fish sauce
1 tablespoon raw sugar or
    palm sugar
2 tablespoons lime juice or to
    taste

1 Peel the pawpaw and shred the flesh very finely – the grating attachment on a food processor will make short work of the job; otherwise use a grater, making the strands as long as possible. String the beans and cut them into bite-sized pieces.

2 Put the dried shrimp in a food processor or blender and grind firmly, then combine with the roasted peanuts.

3 **TO MAKE THE DRESSING**, pound the garlic, shallots, chillies, fish sauce and sugar in a mortar and pestle. Add the beans and pound gently so they don't lose their shape, then the pawpaw shreds. Add the lime juice and toss together. Pile onto a plate and sprinkle over the dried shrimp and peanuts.

# RED CABBAGE SALAD

*Yum Kalum Plee* (Serves 4–6)

1 cup finely sliced onion
1 tablespoon salt
¼ cup dried shrimp
2 cups finely shredded red
   cabbage
2 cups finely shredded green
   or white cabbage
2 teaspoons palm sugar
2–3 tablespoons lime juice
1 teaspoon Pepper and
   Coriander Paste (*page 8*)
2 teaspoons fish sauce or to
   taste
lettuce leaves (garnish)
small whole chillies (garnish)

1 Put the onion in a bowl, rub in the salt, and leave for 20 minutes. Soak the dried shrimp in hot water for 10 minutes and remove any sandy streaks.

2 Lightly pound the drained, soaked shrimp and add 1 cup each of the red and green cabbage. Rinse the salted onions in cold water, drain well, and rub or mix in the sugar, lime juice, Pepper and Coriander Paste and fish sauce.

3 Combine the remaining cabbage with all the ingredients and mix well. Serve on lettuce leaves, garnished with chillies.

# GRILLED EGGPLANT AND DRIED SHRIMP SALAD

*Yum Makua Pao* (Serves 4–6)

*The smoky flavour eggplant acquires when grilled is the distinctive feature of this combination.*

4 slender eggplants
(aubergines)
1 teaspoon finely chopped
garlic
2 teaspoons sugar
½ teaspoon salt
1–2 tablespoons lime juice
1 tablespoon fish sauce
¼ cup dried shrimp
1 red chilli, finely chopped
(garnish)
fresh coriander (garnish)

1 Wash and dry the eggplants. Prick them all over and remove the calyxes. Spear the eggplants on a long fork and hold above a gas flame until charred all over, or cut in half lengthwise and char under the griller (broiler). Set aside until cool enough to handle, then carefully remove the skins and lay the halves on a dish, flat side down.

2 Crush the garlic to a paste with the sugar and salt. Add the lime juice and fish sauce and stir to dissolve the sugar. Taste the dressing – it should be sweet, sour and salty. Sprinkle the eggplants with the dressing, gently lifting the edge of each eggplant half so that the dressing flows underneath.

3 Pick over the dried shrimp, removing any dark spots. In an electric blender or food processor, reduce the shrimp to a floss. Sprinkle over the eggplants, leaving the rounded ends showing. Scatter chopped chilli over and garnish with sprigs of coriander. Serve warm or at room temperature.

# POMELO SALAD

*Yum Som-O* (Serves 4)

*Pomelo may be an unfamiliar fruit in Western countries at present but that looks set to change. It resembles a giant grapefruit and, like grapefruit, there are pink and white varieties. It is now being imported into Australia, and has probably been available in Europe for quite some time – I have seen exotic fruits of many varieties for sale in England, Switzerland and Holland. But don't fret if it has not reached your local market yet, grapefruit is an excellent substitute.*

1 pomelo or 2 grapefruit
1 small clove garlic
1 red chilli, seeded and sliced
1 tablespoon palm sugar
1 tablespoon fish sauce
2 tablespoons lime juice
¼ cup dried shrimp, reduced to a floss in an electric blender
2 tablespoons pea-sized eggplants (aubergines), blanched for 1 minute (optional)
1 stem lemon grass, very finely sliced

1  With a sharp knife peel the fruit, taking off all the thick skin. Divide into segments by cutting between the membranes. Remove any seeds and put the segments in a bowl.

2  Crush the garlic or pound with half of the chilli, palm sugar, fish sauce and lime juice. Mix in the shrimp floss, eggplants if using, and the lemon grass and pour over the pomelo or grapefruit segments in the bowl. Add the remaining chilli slices. Toss gently, then transfer to a serving plate.

# ROSE PETAL SALAD

*Yum Dok Gulab (Serves 4–6)*

*Use fragrant old-fashioned roses, ideally from your own garden. If you get them from anywhere else, be sure the roses have not been sprayed with pesticides. Combine seafood and meats as available, but the main flavours are those of crushed, roasted peanuts, fried garlic and the crisp-fried shallots or sliced onions, readily available from Asian stores.*

4 or 5 roses
1 steamed chicken breast
1 cup small cooked prawns
1 cup cooked pork, thinly
  sliced
2 tablespoons very fine shreds
  of pork skin from Sweet
  Pork (*page 109*)
6 segments pomelo or pink
  grapefruit
¼ cup crushed, roasted
  peanuts
2 teaspoons crisp-fried garlic
1 tablespoon crisp-fried
  shallots
a few leaves of frilly lettuce
slices of cucumber (garnish)

DRESSING
2 tablespoons fish sauce
3 teaspoons sugar
1 tablespoon lime juice
1 fresh red chilli, seeded and
  sliced

1  Wash the roses under a gentle spray of cold water, shake the water from them and place the blossoms, petals downwards, to drain on absorbent paper.

3  With a sharp knife cut the chicken into thin strips. Shell and devein the prawns and, if not very small, cut them into pieces.

3  Combine the chicken and prawns in a bowl with the pork, pork skin, pomelo or grapefruit segments, half of the crushed peanuts, garlic and shallots. Arrange on a plate lined with lettuce and garnish with cucumber.

4  TO MAKE THE DRESSING, stir together the fish sauce, sugar, lime juice and chilli in a small bowl until the sugar dissolves. Spoon the mixture over the combined ingredients and scatter the rose petals over the top. Serve the rest of the peanuts, garlic and fried shallots in a small bowl for sprinkling on top.

# CHICKEN AND CUCUMBER SALAD

*Yum Gai Taeng Gwa* (Serves 4)

*A light and refreshing salad, ideal for dieters.*

250 g (8 oz) chicken breast
1 large or 2 small green
  cucumbers
1 tablespoon dried shrimp
2 tablespoons fish sauce
2 tablespoons lime juice
1–2 teaspoons sugar
2 red chillies, seeded and
  finely sliced
lettuce leaves (garnish)
fresh mint leaves (optional)

1 Steam the chicken breast and when cool, remove the skin and slice the meat.

2 Peel the cucumbers (leave the skin on if not bitter) and slice thinly.

3 In a blender reduce the dried shrimp to a floss.

4 In a small bowl combine the fish sauce, lime juice and sugar, and toss gently with the chicken, cucumber and chilli. Serve on lettuce leaves and sprinkle over the shrimp floss. A few mint leaves may be added, if you like.

# MIXED FRUIT SALAD WITH CHICKEN AND PRAWNS

*Yum Polamai* (Serves 6)

*A salty, sour, lightly hot dressing brings out flavours in familiar fruit that you never dreamed were there! I have used a selection of fruit in season – substitute whichever varieties are available.*

**DRESSING**
**4 tablespoons sugar**
**½ cup (4 fl oz) cold water**
**2 tablespoons fish sauce**
**1 tablespoon lime juice**
**1 red chilli, seeded and sliced**
**1 small clove garlic, crushed**

**a few lettuce leaves**
**1 orange, segmented**
**half a ruby grapefruit,
    segmented**
**half a white grapefruit,
    segmented**
**1 mango, peeled and sliced**
**half a ripe pineapple**
**½ cup water chestnuts, sliced**
**a few miniature tomatoes**
**a few seedless grapes**
**1 cup cooked, sliced chicken**
**1 cup cooked, shelled prawns**
**¼ cup crisp-fried shallots**
**1 teaspoon crisp-fried garlic
    flakes, crushed (*page 208*)**
**¼ cup roasted, salted peanuts,
    crushed**

**1 TO MAKE THE DRESSING**, dissolve the sugar in the cold water, then add the remaining ingredients.

**2** Wash and dry the lettuce leaves and use them to line a serving plate. Place the orange, grapefruit and mango carefully on it.

**3** Using a sharp, stainless steel knife, quarter the pineapple lengthwise and trim off the tough core. Cut across into thin slices. Wash and chill the tomatoes. Wash the grapes and halve them if they are large.

**4** Combine the chicken and prawns in a small bowl and sprinkle a tablespoonful of dressing over, tossing to distribute the flavours. Put the rest of the dressing in the bowl in which it will be served, and place on the platter with the fruits so that each person may spoon some over their portion.

**5** Sprinkle over the shallots, garlic and peanuts just before serving.

# CHIANG MAI CHICKEN SALAD

*Larb Gai Chiang Mai (Serves 4)*

*For convenience, use leftover roast chicken in this recipe – or even ready-cooked barbecued chicken.*

1 large chicken breast
2 stalks lemon grass, thinly
   sliced
2 fresh kaffir lime leaves or
   other tender citrus leaves,
   finely shredded
1 tablespoon roasted rice
   powder (*page 208*)
½ teaspoon chilli powder or
   to taste
2 tablespoons finely sliced
   spring onions, including
   tops
3 tablespoons chopped fresh
   mint leaves
3 tablespoons chopped fresh
   coriander leaves
2 tablespoons fish sauce
4 tablespoons lime juice
1 or 2 red chillies, seeded and
   sliced
1 teaspoon sugar
lettuce leaves
1 tablespoon finely sliced red
   onion
extra mint leaves (garnish)
chilli flower (garnish)

1  Grill (broil) the chicken breast until just cooked through, allow to cool and remove the skin and bones. Chop the meat very finely.

2  Reserve half the lemon grass slices and finely chop the rest.

3  Put the chicken in a bowl and mix with the chopped lemon grass and half the shredded lime leaf, the roasted rice powder, chilli powder, spring onions, mint and coriander.

4  Combine the fish sauce and lime juice, pour half of it over the chicken and toss to mix well.

5  Add the sliced chillies and sugar to the remaining fish sauce and lime juice, stir to dissolve the sugar and serve in a sauce dish alongside the chicken.

6  Arrange the chicken on lettuce leaves and scatter over the reserved sliced lemon grass and red onion. Garnish with mint leaves and a chilli flower. Serve at room temperature.

# BEEF SALAD

## Yum Nuer *(Serves 6)*

*This is probably the most popular salad on Thai restaurant menus. The best flavour comes from barbecuing the steak over coals, but if this is not possible grill (broil) under a preheated griller (broiler).*

500 g (1 lb) rump, fillet or
  sirloin steak
1 teaspoon chopped garlic
1 tablespoon chopped
  coriander roots and stalks
¼ teaspoon freshly ground
  black pepper or 1 teaspoon
  green peppercorns
1 tablespoon palm sugar
2 teaspoons Golden Mountain
  sauce (*page 209*)
1 tablespoon lime juice
2 teaspoons fish sauce
1 cucumber
8 small purple shallots, peeled
  and thinly sliced
3 or 4 red chillies, seeded and
  thinly sliced
1 stem lemon grass, thinly
  sliced
¼ cup fresh mint sprigs
  (garnish)

1  Preheat a griller (broiler) or oven and grill or roast the beef to medium-rare. Allow to cool completely and cut into thin slices.

2  Pound or crush the garlic with the coriander, pepper and palm sugar. Stir in the Golden Mountain sauce, lime juice and fish sauce until blended.

3  Peel the cucumber, score with a fork and slice thinly. Cut in half if the slices are large.

4  Combine all the ingredients except the mint leaves and toss lightly. If preferred, arrange on a platter, garnish with mint and serve the dressing separately.

# CRAB SALAD

*Pla Poo* *(Serves 4)*

*There is no quick and easy way to make a superb crab salad. Sure, you can use frozen or canned crab but it will not look or taste anything like freshly cooked crab.*

2 mudcrabs or 3 blue
   swimmer crabs
2 tablespoons lime juice
2 teaspoons fish sauce
1 small clove garlic
1 teaspoon sugar
3 red chillies, seeded and
   sliced
2 stems lemon grass, thinly
   sliced
2 small shallots, thinly sliced
½ cup fresh mint sprigs
½ cup fresh coriander
lettuce leaves
lime slices (garnish)
red chilli, seeded and finely
   sliced (garnish)

1 If the crabs are already cooked, remove the meat from the shells in pieces as large as possible, picking out any bits of shell and cartilage and discarding the feathery grey tissue underneath the hard top shell or carapace. To cook live crabs, either drop them into boiling water or put them in the freezer for an hour or two. When they have lost consciousness, boil in lightly salted water for 10–15 minutes. Lift out of the water and leave to cool before attempting to crack the claws and pick the meat from the shell.

2 Combine the lime juice and fish sauce. Crush the garlic with the sugar to a smooth paste and stir into the lime juice mixture. If you like, a little of the chilli can be crushed or finely chopped and added to the dressing. Mix well and combine with the crab meat.

3 Add the chillies, lemon grass and shallots, and toss very gently. Add half the mint and coriander.

4 Line a serving plate with washed and dried lettuce leaves and place the crab mixture on top. Garnish with the rest of the mint and coriander, lime slices and chilli.

# CRAB AND WATER CHESTNUT SALAD

*Yum Poo Gub Haeo-Chin* (*Serves 6–8*)

1 cooked crab

1 × 185 g (6 oz) can water
  chestnuts, sliced and cut
  into julienne

1 small onion, finely chopped

2 teaspoons chopped garlic

1 tablespoon peanut oil

2 tablespoons fish sauce

2 tablespoons lime juice

2 teaspoons palm sugar

½ teaspoon finely grated
  kaffir lime rind

1 small hot chilli, seeded and
  finely chopped

250 g (8 oz) cooked prawns
  (shrimp)

250 g (8 oz) finely sliced
  cooked pork

¼ cup roughly chopped fresh
  coriander

3 very tender kaffir lime or
  citrus leaves, finely
  shredded

1  Pick the meat from the crab and put into a bowl.
Combine with the water chesnuts.

2  Fry the onion and 1 teaspoon of the garlic in the oil on
medium heat, stirring so they do not burn. When golden
put them into a small bowl and add the fish sauce, lime
juice, palm sugar, lime rind and chilli. Crush the
remaining teaspoon of garlic and stir in.

3  Shell and devein the prawns and, if large, cut into small
pieces. Combine the prawns and pork with the crab meat,
drizzle the dressing over and toss lightly. Serve sprinkled
with fresh coriander and threads of lime leaf.

# LOBSTER AND MANDARIN SALAD

*Yum Goong Gub Som (Serves 4–6)*

*If lobster is beyond the budget, substitute prawns, seafood flakes or any other delicate seafood in season.*

1 small cooked lobster
50 g (1½ oz) bean starch
   noodles
2 large pieces dried wood
   fungus
2 large mandarins or oranges
3 tablespoons fish sauce
2 tablespoons sugar
2 tablespoons lime juice
1 teaspoon chopped red chilli
¼ cup roasted, crushed
   peanuts
2 tablespoons crisp-fried
   shallots
2 teaspoons crisp-fried garlic
   (optional)
small bunch watercress or
   lettuce
few sprigs of fresh coriander
   (garnish)
chilli flower (garnish)

1 With a sharp knife cut into the lobster from underneath, remove the meat and cut 6 thin slices for garnish. Shred the rest of the lobster meat.

2 Boil the bean starch noodles in lightly salted water for about 10 minutes, until soft and transparent. Drain and cut into short lengths.

3 Soak the wood fungus for 10 minutes in hot water, then cut into fine strips.

4 Peel the mandarins or oranges, divide into segments and remove all the membrane.

5 Put the lobster, noodles and wood fungus into a bowl.

6 Combine the fish sauce, sugar, lime juice and chopped chilli, stirring to dissolve the sugar. Pour over the lobster mixture, add the peanuts and shallots and garlic if using, and toss to distribute the flavours. Taste and add more fish sauce or lime juice if desired. Chill until required.

7 To serve the salad, pile on a platter lined with washed and dried watercress or lettuce. If the lobster is a particularly handsome specimen use the empty shell as a focal point and place the salad alongside. Arrange the reserved lobster slices and mandarin segments on top and garnish with coriander sprigs and a chilli flower.

# SEAFOOD SALAD

*Yum Ta-Leh* (Serves 4)

*The secret to tender seafood is short cooking. Even half a minute too long can be critical, so watch carefully and act quickly! See colour plate on page 61.*

250 g (8 oz) raw prawns
  (shrimp)
250 g (8 oz) cleaned squid
2 kaffir lime leaves
2 sprigs coriander
1 stem lemon grass, finely
  sliced
1 tablespoon fish sauce
2 tablespoons lime juice
2 teaspoons palm sugar
1 teaspoon crushed garlic
1 teaspoon finely chopped
  fresh ginger
½ teaspoon black pepper
½ cup finely sliced spring
  onions, including some
  green tops
¼ cup lightly packed mint
  leaves
2 or 3 fresh red chillies,
  seeded and finely sliced

NOTE *If the squid you buy is very large and might be tough, tenderise it by marinating for a few hours in half a teaspoon bicarbonate of soda (baking soda) dissolved in 3 tablespoons of hot water.*

1 Shell and devein the prawns. Leave the tails on for colour if desired. Slit the squid tubes and rinse. Rub clean with absorbent paper and use a sharp knife to score the inside surface diagonally in parallel lines. Hold the knife at an angle of 45 degrees to achieve deep cuts. Cut the squid into 4 cm (1½ in) strips and then into 5 cm (2 in) pieces.

2 In a small saucepan boil 2 or 3 cups (16–24 fl oz) water with the lime leaves, coriander and lemon grass for 5 minutes. Drop in the squid and as soon as the pieces curl and turn opaque and white, lift out with a slotted spoon (this should take less than a minute). Drop in the prawns until they turn pink, then lift out immediately.

3 Stir together the fish sauce, lime juice, palm sugar, garlic, ginger and pepper. Toss the seafood in the dressing, then add the fresh herbs and chillies and mix lightly.

# PRAWN SALAD IN COCONUT MILK

*Yum Goong Kati* (Serves 4–6)

*A refreshing cold dish to serve either as a first course or with rice and other main dishes.*

12 large raw prawns (jumbo shrimp)

salt

4 tablespoons (3 fl oz) lime juice

1 small red onion, finely sliced

2 red chillies, seeded and sliced

1 cup (8 fl oz) thick coconut milk

1 teaspoon rice flour

1 red chilli, finely shredded (garnish)

2 or 3 fresh kaffir lime leaves, finely shredded (garnish)

1 Shell the prawns, removing all but the last segment of shell and the tail. With a sharp knife slit each along the curve of the back and remove the vein. Rinse the prawns and rub well with salt.

2 Bring a small pan of water to the boil, drop the prawns in and cook for less than 1 minute, or just until they turn opaque and curl.

3 Remove from the heat at once, lift out with a slotted spoon and place in a bowl with the lime juice and a few slices of the onion and chillies. Mix well and set aside until cold.

4 Heat the coconut milk in a small saucepan. Stir in the rice flour mixed with a tablespoon of the coconut milk and cook until it thickens slightly. Pour into a bowl and cool.

5 Drain the liquid from the prawns and stir it into the coconut milk. There should be enough lime juice and salt to season the milk, but if necessary add a pinch of salt and a squeeze of lime juice.

6 Arrange the prawns on a serving plate and pour over the coconut milk dressing. Pile the rest of the onion and chillies in the centre and garnish with chilli and kaffir lime leaves.

# DRIED SHRIMP SALAD WITH LEMON GRASS

*Yum Goong Haeng* (Serves 4)

*A salty, sour, sweet, intriguing combination that goes well with rice and curry. The best dried shrimp is bright salmon pink in colour.*

4 tablespoons dried shrimp
1 tablespoon sugar
4 tablespoons lime juice
1 tablespoon fish sauce
1 stem lemon grass, thinly
   sliced
2 shallots or 1 small purple
   onion, peeled and thinly
   sliced
3 fresh red chillies, seeded and
   sliced
cucumber fan (garnish)

1  Put the dried shrimp in a bowl and pour over enough hot water to cover. Leave to soak until softened, about 10 minutes, then pour off the water. Remove any shrimp with dark veins and discard.

2  Mix the sugar, lime juice and fish sauce together. Combine with all the other ingredients in a bowl and toss to mix. Serve garnished with a cucumber fan.

*Roast duck curry with pineapple (page 98).*

*Barbecued garlic chicken (page 86).*

# COLD BEAN THREAD SALAD

*Yum Woon Sen (Serves 2)*

*The Oriental peanut oil used here is unrefined peanut oil with a distinctive flavour. It is available from Asian food stores.*

50 g (1½ oz) bean starch
   vermicelli
½ teaspoon crushed garlic
2 tablespoons salted peanuts,
   chopped
2 tablespoons fish sauce
1 tablespoon chopped spring
   onions
2 tablespoons chopped fresh
   coriander
juice of half a lime
2 red chillies, seeded and
   finely chopped (optional)
2 teaspoons dried shrimp
   powder
2 teaspoons Oriental peanut
   oil

1 Drop the noodles into boiling water and cook for 10 minutes to soften. Drain in a colander and cut into 2.5 cm (1 in) lengths.

2 Combine with the other ingredients in a bowl and mix well.

# BEAN STARCH NOODLE SALAD WITH WATER CHESTNUTS

*Yum Woon Sen Gub Haeo Chin* (Serves 4–6)

*Because the fine, transparent noodles made of mung bean starch are so difficult to cut when they are dry, I suggest you buy them in 50 g (1½ oz) skeins, usually six to a large pack. It is easy then to use just one small bundle instead of having to cut off a small amount from a large skein.*

50 g (1½ oz) bean starch
　noodles
8–10 dried chillies
⅓ cup dried shrimp
½ teaspoon chopped garlic
½ teaspoon sugar
1 stem lemon grass, finely
　sliced
1 tablespoon fish sauce
2 tablespoons lime juice
2 teaspoons palm sugar
¾ cup sliced water chestnuts
½ cup sliced spring onions
a sprig of basil (garnish)
a sprig of coriander (garnish)

1 Drop the noodles into boiling water and cook for 10 minutes to soften. Drain in a colander and cut into short lengths.

2 Break the tops off the chillies and shake out the seeds. With a pair of scissors, snip the chillies into large pieces, then soak with the dried shrimp in warm water for 10 minutes to soften. Crush the garlic with the sugar.

3 Put the chillies, shrimp, half the lemon grass and garlic in a blender with a little of the chilli-prawn soaking water and blend until smooth. Mix in the fish sauce, lime juice and palm sugar and set aside.

4 Combine the noodles with the water chestnuts, spring onions and the remaining lemon grass. Add the blended shrimp mixture and toss to mix thoroughly. Serve garnished with basil and coriander leaves.

# POULTRY

*C*hicken is commonly found on the menu of the average family, duck more rarely. Poultry in Asian countries are scrawny specimens hanging in unattractive nakedness, in direct contrast to the plump, politely packaged birds the Western shopper buys at the supermarket or butcher. It must also be said that these lean birds are fresh, not frozen and while they require longer cooking to become tender, they have more flavour. I think most city dwellers in Western countries have forgotten – if they ever knew – what chicken should taste like.

If you have access to fresh, free-range chickens they are obviously ideal, but all our recipes were tested with readily available supermarket roasting chickens. Cooking the Thai way with clever use of herbs and spices is an ideal way to compensate for lack of flavour in the poultry.

# STUFFED CHICKEN WINGS

*Peek Gai Yud Sai (Serves 6–8)*

*Not as difficult as it sounds, especially if you buy medium-sized wings. Large wings with well-developed sinews holding the bones in place require more effort. A small, sharp, pointed knife carefully used is invaluable.*

12 chicken wings
250 g (8 oz) minced (ground)
    pork
1 teaspoon sugar
2 tablespoons fish sauce
½ cup finely chopped spring
    onions
2 teaspoons Pepper and
    Coriander Paste (*page 8*)
30 g (1 oz) bean starch
    noodles, soaked and sliced
    into 2.5 cm (1 in) lengths
¾ cup (3 oz) rice flour
peanut oil for frying
Peanut Sauce (*page 56*)
2 fresh kaffir lime leaves,
    finely shredded (garnish)
1 red chilli, finely shredded
    (garnish)

COCONUT TOPPING
¾ cup (6 fl oz) coconut milk
1 teaspoon rice flour
½ teaspoon salt

1 Cut the chicken wings at the first joint and keep the top joint for use in another dish. To remove the two bones in the wing, place the point of a knife between them and run the knife around the top of each bone. Push the flesh down and off the bone and carefully twist each bone out.

2 Place the pork in a food processor with the sugar, fish sauce, spring onions, and Pepper and Coriander Paste. Process until smooth, then remove from the processor and mix in the drained bean starch noodles. Fill the boned section of the wings with 1–2 teaspoons of filling each. Do not overfill or they will burst when steamed. Secure the tops with a small skewer. (Two wings would fit on each skewer.)

3 Steam over boiling water for 6 or 7 minutes, then leave to cool. Dust with rice flour, deep-fry in hot oil and drain on absorbent paper.

4 FOR THE COCONUT TOPPING, bring the coconut milk, rice flour and salt gently to the boil, stirring until the coconut milk thickens. Spoon the topping over the chicken wings followed by the Peanut Sauce. Garnish with shreds of lime leaf and chilli. Serve at room temperature.

# CHICKEN SALAD WITH VEGETABLES

*Yum Tha Wai* (Serves 4–6)

*An easy dish to prepare, ideal to do ahead.*

SAUCE

4 or 5 dried chillies, seeded

½ cup dried shrimp

2 tablespoons sesame seeds,
   toasted

4 tablespoons desiccated
   coconut, toasted

2 whole heads pickled garlic,
   chopped

¾ cup (6 fl oz) thick coconut
   milk

2 tablespoons palm sugar

2 tablespoons fish sauce

1 tablespoon lime juice

1 tablespoon dried tamarind,
   soaked in ½ cup (4 fl oz)
   hot water and strained

1 tablespoon crisp-fried
   shallots (garnish)

TOPPING

½ cup (4 fl oz) thick coconut
   milk

1 teaspoon rice flour

½ teaspoon salt

1 whole chicken breast,
   steamed

3 cups mixed vegetables

1 **TO MAKE THE SAUCE,** break the dried chillies into pieces and soak in a little boiling water for 10 minutes until softened. Soak the dried shrimp in just enough hot water to cover for 10 minutes.

2 Reserve a tablespoon each of the sesame seeds and desiccated coconut for the garnish, and crush the remainder in a mortar and pestle or put into the container of an electric blender. Add the drained chillies, shrimp and pickled garlic and grind everything finely, adding a little coconut milk if necessary to facilitate blending.

3 Heat the thick coconut milk until oily and add the blended mixture. Cook for a few minutes, stirring well. Stir in the palm sugar, fish sauce, lime juice and tamarind liquid. Simmer to reduce and thicken the sauce.

4 **TO MAKE THE TOPPING,** heat the thick coconut milk, rice flour and salt in another pan, stirring, until it boils and thickens.

5 Slice the chicken breast into strips.

6 Blanch the vegetables until just half-cooked, then drain and refresh in ice water for a few minutes to stop the cooking. Drain again. Arrange the vegetables on a platter and place the chicken strips on top.

7 Just before serving spoon on first the sauce and finally the topping. Sprinkle with the fried shallots, and the reserved toasted coconut and sesame seeds.

# BARBECUED GARLIC CHICKEN

*Gai Yang (Serves 6)*

*This versatile recipe may be used with chicken pieces such as thighs or half-breasts, or a boned half-chicken which makes serving easy – it is simply sliced through, the only bone left being in the wing. See colour plate on page 80.*

1.5 kg (3 lb) roasting chicken
   or chicken pieces
3 teaspoons chopped garlic
2 teaspoons salt
2 tablespoons black
   peppercorns, crushed
1 cup finely chopped fresh
   coriander, including roots
2 tablespoons lime juice
tomatoes (garnish)
spring onion curls (garnish)

1 Cut the chicken in half lengthwise, and if you like, remove the bones with a small, pointed knife, leaving only the wing bones.

2 Crush the garlic with the salt to a smooth purée. Combine the peppercorns in a flat dish with the coriander and the lime juice. Rub the mixture well into the chicken on all sides, cover and refrigerate overnight, or at least 1 hour.

3 Since a boned chicken does not stay in shape as well as one with the bones in, use poultry skewers to hold it firm and make it easy to turn while cooking. Barbecue over glowing coals, approximately 15 cm (6 in) from the heat. Cook, turning every 5 minutes or so, until the chicken is no longer pink and the skin is crisp. If the weather doesn't permit barbecuing, cook under a preheated griller (broiler).

4 To serve a boned chicken, place the halves skin side upward on a platter or board and slice with a sharp knife into diagonal slices. If the chicken is not boned, separate into joints. Garnish with tomatoes and curls of spring onion. Serve with a salad of sliced cucumber, spring onions and tomatoes seasoned with lime juice and salt.

# FRIED CHICKEN WITH BASIL

*Phad Gai Bai Kraprao* (Serves 4)

1 tablespoon peanut oil

1½ teaspoons finely chopped
   garlic

1 tablespoon shredded fresh
   ginger

250 g (8 oz) chicken breast
   fillets, sliced

½ cup shredded bamboo
   shoots

4 fresh red chillies, seeded and
   finely sliced

1 tablespoon fish sauce

1 tablespoon Golden
   Mountain sauce (*page 209*)
   or oyster sauce

1 teaspoon sugar

4 spring onions, sliced

½ cup sweet basil leaves

1  Heat the oil in a wok and fry the garlic and ginger until golden. Add the chicken and stir-fry for 3 or 4 minutes.

2  Add the bamboo shoots, chillies, the sauces, sugar and spring onions. Simmer 3 minutes longer, stir in the basil leaves and serve with steamed jasmine rice or noodles.

# CHICKEN CURRY

*Kaeng Gai* *(Serves 6)*

*This curry doesn't use any of the pastes, but has a special combination of spices that is very individual.*

3 or 4 dried chillies, seeded
   and sliced
1 small onion, chopped
2 teaspoons chopped garlic
1 teaspoon chopped galangal
1 teaspoon chopped lemon
   grass or zest of 1 lemon
1 teaspoon chopped coriander
   root
½ teaspoon shredded kaffir
   lime rind
1 teaspoon salt
1 teaspoon dried shrimp paste
¼ teaspoon peppercorns
2 tablespoons peanut oil
500 g (1 lb) chicken thigh
   fillets, cut into bite-sized
   pieces
1 cup (8 fl oz) coconut milk
1 tablespoon fish sauce
1 tablespoon palm sugar
3 kaffir lime leaves
20 fresh sweet basil leaves

1 Pound the chillies and onion to a paste in a mortar and pestle, adding the garlic, galangal, lemon grass or lemon zest, coriander root, lime rind, salt, shrimp paste and peppercorns. Or put into a blender and grind until smooth, adding 1 tablespoon of the oil to facilitate blending.

2 Heat a wok, add 1 tablespoon of oil and fry the pounded mixture, stirring constantly, until oil appears on the surface.

3 Add the chicken and stir-fry until it changes colour, then stir in the coconut milk, fish sauce, palm sugar and kaffir lime leaves. Simmer until the chicken is tender.

4 Add the sweet basil leaves just before whisking it off the heat and serve with steamed jasmine rice.

# CHICKEN IN SPICY PEANUT SAUCE

*Gai Phad Sauce Tua* (Serves 6)

*When you have a supply of curry pastes, a dish like this can be made in less than half an hour.*

1 kg (2 lb) chicken half-
　breasts
1 teaspoon crushed garlic
2 teaspoons finely grated fresh
　ginger
1 tablespoon Red Curry Paste
　(*page 3*)
2 tablespoons peanut oil
1 cup spring onions, cut into
　5 cm (2 in) lengths
¼ cup roasted peanuts,
　crushed or 2 tablespoons
　crunchy peanut butter
2 teaspoons palm sugar
1 tablespoon fish sauce
1 cup (8 fl oz) coconut milk
2 cups broccoli florets

1 Cut each half-breast in half again with a sharp chopper. Wash them to get rid of any splinters of bone, and dry well on paper towels.

2 Combine the garlic, ginger and Red Curry Paste and rub well over the chicken pieces. Set aside for about 20 minutes.

3 Heat a wok, pour in the oil and swirl to coat the wok. Toss the spring onions in the oil for a few seconds, remove and set aside. Fry the chicken pieces, turning them over until browned all over.

4 Add the peanuts or peanut butter, palm sugar, fish sauce and coconut milk. Stir well to combine. Cover and simmer until the chicken is tender. If the sauce reduces too much add a little water and stir well.

5 Blanch the broccoli florets in boiling water for 2 minutes. Drain. Add the broccoli and spring onions to the chicken and mix gently. Serve hot with steamed jasmine rice and a tangy salad.

# CHICKEN WITH BEANS

*Gai Phad Tua* (Serves 4)

*A simple stir-fried combination with the favourite flavours of Thai cuisine.*

250 g (8 oz) green beans, cut
   into 5 cm (2 in) lengths
1 tablespoon finely sliced
   lemon grass or zest of
   1 lemon
2 teaspoons chopped fresh
   ginger
2 or 3 fresh chillies, seeded
   and sliced
½ teaspoon grated kaffir lime
   rind
½ teaspoon black pepper
1 teaspoon garlic, finely
   chopped
1 tablespoon peanut oil
250 g (8 oz) chicken fillets,
   breast or thigh, sliced
¼ cup (2 fl oz) coconut cream
¼ teaspoon salt
shredded lettuce or cabbage
1 fresh lime leaf, shredded
   (garnish)
extra sliced chillies (optional)

1 Blanch the beans in boiling water until just cooked, drain and refresh in ice water.

2 In a mortar and pestle pound the lemon grass, ginger, chillies, lime rind, pepper and garlic to a paste. Mix with the chicken, cover and set aside for 10–15 minutes.

3 Heat the oil in a wok and stir-fry the chicken on medium-high heat until it changes colour, about 3 or 4 minutes. Add the beans and stir-fry for a further minute or two until heated through.

4 Heat the coconut cream and salt and spoon over the chicken. Serve on a bed of shredded lettuce or tender cabbage. Garnish with shreds of lime leaf and extra sliced chillies, if desired.

# CHICKEN AND BAMBOO SHOOT CURRY

*Kaeng Phed Gai Nor Mai* (Serves 4)

½ cup (4 fl oz) thick coconut
  milk
1½ tablespoons Red Curry
  Paste (*page 3*)
300 g (10 oz) chicken breast
  fillet, sliced into strips
1 tablespoon finely sliced
  lemon grass
2 kaffir lime leaves, fresh,
  frozen or dried
1 cup (8 fl oz) thin coconut
  milk
1 piece canned bamboo shoot,
  sliced into bite-sized pieces
2 or 3 fresh red chillies,
  seeded and sliced
1 tablespoon fish sauce
1 tablespoon palm sugar
20 fresh basil leaves
½ cup sliced spring onions

1 Heat the thick coconut milk in a wok and cook the Red Curry Paste, stirring, until fragrant. Add the sliced chicken, lemon grass and lime leaves and cook for 2 or 3 minutes, stirring to coat the chicken with the mixture.

2 Add the thin coconut milk and bamboo shoots and simmer, uncovered, for about 7 minutes. Stir in all the remaining ingredients and cook for 1 minute longer. Serve hot with steamed jasmine rice or noodles.

# CHICKEN AND STRAW MUSHROOM CURRY

*Phad Phed Gai Hed Farng* (Serves 4)

1 cup straw mushrooms

2 tablespoons peanut oil

3 tablespoons finely chopped
spring onions

½ teaspoon finely chopped
garlic

1 tablespoon Red Curry Paste
(*page 3*)

2 fresh red chillies, seeded and
chopped

250 g (8 oz) chicken thigh
fillets, diced

1 tablespoon fish sauce

½ cup (4 fl oz) thick coconut
milk

2 fresh kaffir lime leaves,
finely shredded (garnish)

1 If fresh straw mushrooms are used, trim each base, cut the mushrooms in half lengthwise and blanch in boiling water for 1 minute. Drain. If using canned straw mushrooms, drain the liquid away and cut the mushrooms in half.

2 Heat a wok, add the oil and when it is hot stir in the spring onions, garlic, curry paste and chillies. Cook, stirring, for 2 minutes or until fragrant. Add the diced chicken and stir-fry until it changes colour.

3 Stir in the mushrooms, fish sauce and coconut milk, and cook for a few minutes longer, uncovered, on medium-low heat. Serve sprinkled with lime leaves and accompanied by steamed jasmine rice.

# CHICKEN FILLET WITH SNOW PEAS

*Kaeng Khiew Wan Gai Tua* (Serves 4)

300 g (10 oz) chicken thigh
   fillets
100 g (3½ oz) snow peas
   (*mange-tout*)
1 cup (8 fl oz) coconut milk
2 tablespoons Green Curry
   Paste (*page 4*)
1 tablespoon fish sauce
½ cup water
4 kaffir lime leaves, shredded
1 or 2 fresh green chillies,
   seeded and sliced
20 sweet basil leaves

1 Cut the chicken into bite-sized pieces. String the snow peas and set aside.

2 In a wok, heat ½ cup (4 fl oz) of the coconut milk and when it is bubbling add the Green Curry Paste and stir over medium heat until fragrant.

3 Add the fish sauce and chicken pieces and stir constantly until the chicken is coated with the mixture and is no longer pink.

4 Mix the remaining coconut milk with the water and add to the pan with the kaffir lime leaves and chillies. Simmer gently for 15 minutes, stir in the snow peas and basil leaves, and simmer for 5 minutes longer. Serve with steamed jasmine rice.

# CHICKEN AND SATAW NUTS

*Gai Phad Sataw* (Serves 4–6)

*This is a dish from southern Thailand where sataw (also spelled 'sator') nuts are very popular. Though called nuts, they are the soft, fresh green seeds of a giant bean. They have a distinctive bitter flavour, which could take a little getting used to, and are available bottled in brine, or in cans under the name petai.*

250 g (8 oz) chicken thigh
    fillets
1 teaspoon crushed garlic
¼ teaspoon whole black
    peppercorns
½ cup chopped coriander,
    including roots
small piece fresh turmeric root
    or ½ teaspoon ground
    turmeric
¼ teaspoon salt
1 teaspoon *Tom Yum* Paste
    (*page 6*)
2 tablespoons peanut oil
250 g (8 oz) fresh asparagus,
    cut into 2.5 cm (1 in)
    lengths
100 g (3½ oz) snow peas
    (*mange-tout*), strung
¼ cup drained sataw nuts
1 or 2 fresh green chillies,
    seeded and finely sliced
1 tablespoon fish sauce or to
    taste
2 cups (16 fl oz) coconut milk
20 sweet basil leaves
2 tablespoons fresh coriander
    leaves

1 Trim every bit of skin and fat from the chicken fillets and cut the meat into very thin shreds.

2 Pound the garlic, peppercorns, coriander and turmeric with a mortar and pestle to a paste.

3 Add the salt and paste and marinate the chicken in this mixture for at least 1 hour.

4 Heat a wok, add the oil and swirl around in the wok. Add the marinated chicken and stir-fry over high heat until the chicken changes colour.

5 Add the asparagus, snow peas, sataw nuts, chillies and fish sauce. Add the coconut milk, stirring constantly, until the vegetables are cooked.

6 Toss in the basil and coriander leaves and simmer, uncovered, for 5–10 minutes. Serve with steamed jasmine rice.

# CHICKEN WITH GINGER AND WOOD FUNGUS

*Gai Phad Khing Hed Hung (Serves 4)*

*When ginger is young the skin is almost transparent and the tips of the rhizome are pink – perfect for using generously in recipes like this because it is not too pungent. If more mature ginger is all that is available, halve the amount and soak it in lightly salted water for 10 minutes. Dry on absorbent paper before using.*

4 medium-sized chicken
   breast or thigh fillets
¼ cup dried wood fungus
¼ cup finely shredded ginger
2 tablespoons peanut oil
1 white onion, thinly sliced
1 teaspoon finely chopped
   garlic
1 tablespoon light soy sauce
1 tablespoon fish sauce
1 tablespoon rice vinegar
1 teaspoon palm sugar or
   brown sugar
¼ cup chopped spring onions
   (garnish)
¼ cup chopped fresh
   coriander (garnish)

1 Dice the chicken, discarding any skin or bone.

2 Rinse the wood fungus and soak in hot water for 10 minutes, or until it is soft. Drain, discard any gritty portions and cut the fungus into bite-sized pieces.

3 To cut shreds of ginger, rub off the skin if tender enough, or peel thinly with a potato peeler. Slice very thinly lengthwise, stack a few slices at a time and cut into thin shreds.

4 Heat the oil and fry the onion until soft and translucent. Add the garlic and stir-fry until golden. Add the chicken and ginger, tossing until the chicken changes colour.

5 Stir in the soy sauce, fish sauce, vinegar and sugar. As soon as the liquid boils, lower the heat, cover and simmer for 3 minutes. Do not overcook. Serve sprinkled with spring onions and fresh coriander.

# CHICKEN AND VEGETABLES WITH CHILLI-SHRIMP SAUCE

*Gai, Pak Phad, Nam Prik* (Serves 6)

500 g (1 lb) chicken thighs
3 cups mixed vegetables such
    as green beans, asparagus,
    bamboo shoots,
    bean sprouts
4 or 5 dried red chillies,
    seeded
½ cup dried shrimp
3 cloves garlic
1½ cups (12 fl oz) thick
    coconut milk
2 tablespoons palm sugar or
    brown sugar
2 tablespoons fish sauce
1 tablespoon lime juice
1 tablespoon tamarind pulp
¼ cup crushed, roasted
    peanuts (garnish)

TOPPING
½ cup (4 fl oz) thick coconut
    milk
½ teaspoon salt
1 teaspoon rice flour

1 Steam or poach the chicken until cooked, allow to cool then cut into thick slices, discarding the bones.

2 Blanch each vegetable separately in lightly salted boiling water until tender but still crisp. Refresh in ice water to stop the cooking and set the colour. Drain.

3 Soak the chillies and dried shrimp in hot water for 10 minutes to soften, then drain. Chop the chillies and pound to a paste with the shrimp and garlic in a mortar and pestle.

4 Heat ½ cup (4 fl oz) of the coconut milk until it separates and add the pounded mixture. Stir in the palm sugar, fish sauce, lime juice and tamarind. Cook until syrupy and gradually stir in the remaining cup of coconut milk and simmer to reduce. The sauce will darken as it reduces.

5 TO MAKE THE TOPPING, heat the coconut milk, salt and rice flour in a small pan, stirring, until it thickens.

6 Arrange the prepared vegetables on a serving plate, place the sliced chicken on top and spoon over the sauce, followed by the topping. Sprinkle with toasted peanuts and serve at once.

# CHILLI CHICKEN WITH NOODLES

*Kway Teo Phad (Serves 4)*

*A good example of how a little meat or poultry can go a long way towards flavouring a whole dish of noodles when spiced up with chillies and garlic.*

250 g (8 oz) boneless chicken
4 tablespoons peanut oil
2 dried red chillies
1 tablespoon garlic flakes
½ cup peanuts
1 tablespoon Red Curry Paste
   (*page 3*)
¼ cup (2 fl oz) water
2 tablespoons chilli sauce
   (optional)
2 tablespoons fish sauce
220 g (7 oz) rice noodles,
   cooked and drained
2 tablespoons lime juice
½ cup sliced spring onions
½ cup chopped fresh
   coriander (garnish)

1  Remove the skin and excess fat from the chicken and cut the meat into strips.

2  Heat the oil, fry the dried chillies on medium heat until they are puffed up and blackened, then remove to absorbent paper. Remove the stalks from the chillies, shake out the seeds and chop them into small pieces.

3  Fry the garlic flakes on low heat for just a few seconds. Lift them out on a large wire strainer as soon as they turn pale golden, as they will continue to cook in their own heat. Drain.

4  Add the peanuts and stir constantly until they are light brown. Lift out and allow to cool on absorbent paper.

5  Crush the garlic flakes and peanuts. Mix all three together for sprinkling over the dish at the end.

6  If necessary, add an extra tablespoon of oil to the wok and fry the Red Curry Paste, stirring, for a couple of minutes. Add the chicken and stir-fry on medium-high heat until it changes colour.

7  Add the water, chilli sauce if using, and the fish sauce. Boil for 1 minute, then add the noodles, lime juice and spring onions, and toss in the spicy mixture until heated through. Sprinkle with the peanut mixture and fresh coriander. Extra fish sauce and lime juice mixed with sliced hot chillies may accompany the noodles for real chilli devotees.

# ROAST DUCK CURRY WITH PINEAPPLE

*Kaeng Phed Ped Yang Subparot* (Serves 4)

*A quick, easy and not-too-hot curry, fragrant with basil and citrus leaves. Rather than go to the trouble of roasting a duck, purchase one ready-cooked from an Asian store. See colour plate on page 79.*

½ a roast duck
½ a pineapple
6 fresh or dried kaffir lime
    leaves, left whole
1 x 400 ml (13 fl oz) can
    coconut milk or 2 cups
    (16 fl oz) fresh coconut
    milk
1–2 teaspoons Red Curry Paste
    (*page 3*)
1 cup (8 fl oz) water
2 fresh red chillies or small
    capsicums, seeded
1 cup sliced canned bamboo
    shoot, cut into bite-sized
    pieces
2 tablespoons fish sauce
20 fresh basil leaves
2 teaspoons palm sugar

1 Chop the duck into pieces through the bone, or remove the bones and cut the meat into bite-sized pieces.

2 Peel and core the pineapple, remove the 'eyes' and cut the flesh into bite-sized pieces.

3 If using dried lime leaves, soak them in a little hot water. Leave four leaves whole and finely shred the other two after removing the tough centre rib.

4 Heat ½ cup (4 fl oz) of the canned coconut milk or the first extract of fresh coconut in a pan, and when bubbling, stir in the curry paste. Fry, stirring, until it becomes oily.

5 Add the duck and toss with the curry mixture, then add another ½ cup of coconut milk and the water.

6 Add the pineapple, bamboo shoots, lime leaves, chillies and fish sauce. Simmer for 10–15 minutes until the sauce has reduced and thickened.

7 Add the basil leaves and palm sugar, stirring to dissolve the sugar. Finally, stir in the rest of the coconut milk and sprinkle over the shredded lime leaves. Serve with steamed jasmine rice.

# DUCK WITH LYCHEES

*Kaeng Ped Linjee (Serves 4–6)*

500 g (1 lb) shredded duck
    meat, skin and bones
    removed
2 cups (16 fl oz) coconut milk
3 kaffir lime leaves
2 tablespoons fish sauce or to
    taste
5 large dried chillies, seeded
2 teaspoons finely chopped
    fresh galangal or
    1 teaspoon ground
2 tablespoons finely sliced
    lemon grass or zest of
    1 lemon
½ teaspoon finely grated
    kaffir lime rind
1 tablespoon chopped
    coriander roots
3 teaspoons chopped garlic
½ teaspoon black peppercorns
1 teaspoon dried shrimp paste
2 cups (16 fl oz) thick coconut
    milk
2 teaspoons palm sugar
3 tablespoons crushed, roasted
    peanuts or crunchy peanut
    butter
¼ cup pea-sized eggplants
    (aubergines) (optional)
½ cup lightly packed basil
    leaves
1 tablespoon sliced hot red
    chillies
1 cup (1 x 570 g/1 lb 2 oz can)
    lychees, drained
1 tablespoon lime juice
1 teaspoon salt or to taste
lime leaf, shredded

1 Simmer the duck in the coconut milk with the lime leaves and fish sauce until the meat is tender.

2 Break the chillies in pieces and pour a little boiling water over. Leave to soak for 10 minutes.

3 Put the drained chillies, galangal, lemon grass, lime rind, coriander roots, garlic, peppercorns and shrimp paste in a mortar and pound to a paste. Alternatively, grind in an electric blender, using a little water from the soaked chillies to facilitate blending.

4 Set aside ½ cup (4 fl oz) of the thick coconut milk. Put the rest in a wok or saucepan and bring to the boil, stirring constantly. When thick and oily add the ground ingredients and simmer, stirring constantly, until thick and fragrant.

5 Add the palm sugar and peanuts or peanut butter and mix well. Stir in the eggplants if using, and the drained duck meat. Continue simmering for 10 minutes, then add the basil leaves. Reserve 1 teaspoon of the sliced chillies and add the remainder to the curry. Cook a couple of minutes longer, adding some of the liquid in which the duck was cooked.

6 Toss the lychees with the lime juice and salt, and stir in when the mixture has reduced and thickened. Serve topped with the reserved thick coconut milk and garnished with the remaining sliced chillies and a few shreds of lime leaf. Serve with steamed jasmine rice.

# DUCK MASAMAN CURRY

*Masaman Ped* (Serves 4)

*This is a Muslim-style curry, featuring the fragrant spices that denote an Indian influence, but somehow tempered with the special flavours of Thailand – a true hybrid.*

1 cup (8 fl oz) thick coconut
  milk
3 tablespoons Masaman Curry
  Paste (*page 5*)
1 kg (2 lb) duck, cut into bite-
  sized pieces
1 cup (8 fl oz) thin coconut
  milk
3 kaffir lime leaves
1 tablespoon palm sugar
5 cardamom pods, bruised
1 cup pea-sized eggplants
  (aubergines) (optional)
2 tablespoons ground roasted
  peanuts or crunchy peanut
  butter
2 tablespoons fish sauce
2 tablespoons tamarind liquid
1 tablespoon lime juice
fresh coriander leaves
  (garnish)

**1** Heat ½ cup (4 fl oz) of the thick coconut milk until oily and stir in the Masaman Curry Paste. Cook, stirring constantly, until fragrant.

**2** Stir in the duck pieces, thin coconut milk, lime leaves, palm sugar and cardamom pods. Simmer 30–45 minutes, or until almost tender.

**3** Stir in the eggplants, if using, peanuts or peanut butter and the remaining ½ cup thick coconut milk and cook for 10 minutes longer.

**4** Add the fish sauce, tamarind liquid and lime juice. The sauce should be slightly reduced. Garnish with coriander and serve with steamed jasmine rice.

# SON-IN-LAW EGGS

*Kai Look Koei* (Serves 6)

6 eggs
¼ cup (2 fl oz) peanut oil
1 medium onion, thinly sliced
2 fresh chillies, seeded and
   sliced
2 tablespoons palm sugar
3 tablespoons water
2 teaspoons instant tamarind
   pulp
1 tablespoon fish sauce
chilli flower (garnish)
coriander leaves (garnish)

1 Place the eggs into boiling water, stirring gently to centre the yolks. Simmer for 8 minutes, then run cold water into the pan until they are quite cold. Shell the eggs and wipe dry on absorbent paper. Pierce each one 2 or 3 times with a very fine toothpick.

2 Heat the oil in a wok and fry the eggs until golden and crisp. Drain on absorbent paper. Pour off all but a tablespoon of the oil. Stir-fry the onion and chillies until the onions turn golden and are slightly crisp. Drain.

3 Mix the palm sugar, water, tamarind and fish sauce. Stir over low heat for 5 minutes or until slightly thick. Pour the sauce over the eggs, sprinkle the fried onion and chillies over, and garnish with a chilli flower and coriander leaves. Serve with steamed jasmine rice.

# GRILLED SPICED QUAIL

*Nok-Krata Yang* (Serves 4–8)

8 dressed quail
2 teaspoons Pepper and
   Coriander Paste (*page 8*)
2 teaspoons Red Curry Paste
   (*page 3*)
2 teaspoons Sweet Chilli Sauce
   (*page 54*)
1 teaspoon Golden Mountain
   sauce (*page 209*) or light soy
   sauce
1 tablespoon honey
1 tablespoon peanut oil

1 Wash and dry the quail and truss them, holding the legs together with a poultry skewer. Combine the rest of the ingredients and brush over the birds. Marinate for at least an hour.

2 Preheat a griller (broiler). Dry the birds on paper towels if they become wet, and brush again with the remaining marinade. Grill over glowing coals or under a griller (broiler) at a good distance from the heat so the birds are cooked through. While cooking, brush them with a little oil mixed with the remaining marinade.

# MEAT

The newcomer to Thai food may take one look at the recipes in this chapter and think I'm skimping on portions! However, in Thailand meat is never eaten in large amounts; rice is the mainstay of the meal. Meat is often cooked with the marvellous flavours of herbs and spices, often with a rich coconut sauce, and a little meat is eaten with a large amount of rice.

Don't be surprised to find meat combined with seafood in certain recipes, for instance in the Pork and Crab Sausage (page 117). It may sound strange, but is actually quite delicious!

# MIXED SATAY

*(Serves 4–6)*

*Some of the nicest satays I have tasted were at a little family-run noodle shop in Chiang Mai. They were distinctly sweet, and the lady making them said they were marinated only briefly. The skewers on which the satays are grilled should be soaked in water overnight or for at least 2 hours to prevent them burning.*

500 g (8 oz) boneless chicken,
    beef or pork
2 tablespoons peanut oil
1 tablespoon finely sliced
    lemon grass
1 red chilli, seeded and sliced
2 teaspoons chopped garlic
1 teaspoon palm sugar
2 teaspoons fish sauce
bamboo skewers

1 Trim the meat of any excess fat and remove the chicken skin. Slice the meat and cut into 5 cm (2 in) long strips.

2 In an electric blender combine the oil, lemon grass, chilli, garlic, palm sugar and fish sauce on high speed to make a purée. Pour over the meat and mix well. Marinate for at least 2 hours. Preheat a grill (broiler) or barbecue.

3 Thread 2 or 3 pieces of marinated meat onto each skewer and cook on the barbecue or under a grill (broiler), turning 2 or 3 times. The meat should be well done but not overcooked. Serve with Peanut Sauce (*page 56*) and Chilli and Cucumber Salad (*page 60*).

# RED PORK CURRY WITH YOUNG CORN

*Kaeng Phed Moo Kao Poad Orn* (Serves 4–6)

*See colour plate on page 113.*

1 tablespoon peanut oil

3 tablespoons Red Curry Paste
  (*page 3*)

500 g (1 lb) lean pork, diced

1½ cups (12 fl oz) coconut
  milk

½ teaspoon grated kaffir lime
  rind

2 or 3 kaffir lime leaves

2 tablespoons fish sauce

10 fresh basil leaves

1 or 2 red chillies, seeded and
  sliced

1 × 425 g can young corn
  cobs, drained

3 or 4 fresh kaffir lime or
  citrus leaves, shredded
  (garnish)

red chillies, seeded and sliced
  (garnish)

1 Heat the oil in a wok or saucepan and fry the curry paste until fragrant. Add the pork and stir-fry until it changes colour. Stir in the coconut milk, lime rind and leaves. Stir until boiling.

2 Reduce the heat and simmer for 35 minutes or until the pork is tender, stirring occasionally and adding extra coconut milk if necessary.

3 When the pork is very tender, stir in the fish sauce, basil leaves, chillies and corn and cook for a further 5 minutes. Serve with steamed jasmine rice and garnish with kaffir lime leaves and chillies.

# PORK CURRY WITH GINGER AND PICKLED GARLIC

*Moo Phad Khing Kratiem Dong (Serves 4–6)*

*A robust-flavoured dish for those who don't flinch from garlic at full strength.*

½ **cup finely shredded fresh ginger**
1 **tablespoon sliced fresh garlic**
1 **onion, chopped**
2 **tablespoons Red Curry Paste** (*page 3*)
1 **teaspoon ground turmeric**
1 **teaspoon finely grated kaffir lime rind**
750 **g (1½ lb) loin of pork, cut into 5 cm (2 in) squares**
3 **tablespoons peanut oil**
2 **tablespoons fish sauce**
5 **fresh or dried kaffir lime leaves**
1 **tablespoon dried tamarind pulp**
2 **tablespoons sliced pickled garlic**
2 **teaspoons palm sugar**

---

**NOTE** *This curry is even nicer when prepared a couple of days before serving. Cool, cover tightly and store in the refrigerator.*

---

1  Put half the shredded ginger into a small bowl of salted water and leave to soak. Put the remaining ginger, all the fresh garlic and onion into a mortar and pestle and pound, or into a blender and whiz to a smooth purée.

2  Mix with the curry paste, turmeric and kaffir lime rind. Marinate the pork in this mixture for about 20 minutes.

3  Heat a wok or saucepan and pour in the oil. When the oil is hot fry the pork, stirring, until the colour changes.

4  Add the fish sauce, lime leaves, and the reserved ginger shreds drained from the soaking water.

5  Dissolve the tamarind pulp in 1 cup (8 fl oz) of hot water, strain and add, stirring well. Cover and simmer until the pork is tender. Stir in the pickled garlic and palm sugar, simmer a minute or two longer and serve hot with steamed jasmine rice and accompaniments.

# PORK PANANG CURRY

*Panang Moo* (Serves 4–6)

500 g (1 lb) belly pork
1 tablespoon fish sauce
1 tablespoon palm sugar
¼ cup pea-sized eggplants
   (aubergines) (optional)
1½ cups (12 fl oz) coconut
   milk
3 tablespoons Panang Curry
   Paste *(page 7)*
½ cup sliced bamboo shoot
15–20 basil leaves
red chilli, shredded (garnish)
lime leaves, shredded
   (garnish)

1 Cut the belly pork into strips 2 cm (¾ in) wide and 4 cm (1½ in) long and place in a saucepan with the fish sauce and palm sugar and just enough water to cover. Simmer until the meat is tender and the rind is clear. Drain and retain the stock.

2 Blanch and drain the eggplants if using. Heat half of the coconut milk, add the curry paste and simmer until fragrant.

3 Stir in the pork and cook until the oil separates from the gravy. Add the eggplant and bamboo shoots and simmer for 10 minutes, adding a little pork stock if necessary. Shortly before serving, stir in the basil leaves. Spoon the remaining coconut milk over and garnish with shreds of red chilli and lime leaves.

# PORK WITH BITTER GOURD

*Khiew Wan Mara Yud Sai Moo (Serves 6)*

*Undoubtedly bitter gourd, or bitter melon as it is sometimes called, is an acquired taste. Those who have grown accustomed to it relish it immensely, and eat it fried, cooked in coconut milk, or even raw as a salad. My favourite way is thinly sliced gourd sprinkled with salt and turmeric and left for an hour, then wiped over and shallow-fried until golden brown. Choose slender, deep-green gourds. Those which are turning yellow and are too plump indicate over-ripeness.*

**PORK FILLING**
250 g (8 oz) minced (ground) pork
1 teaspoon sugar
1 teaspoon finely grated fresh ginger
1 teaspoon crushed garlic
1 tablespoon finely chopped spring onions
1 tablespoon finely chopped fresh coriander
1 teaspoon Green Curry Paste *(page 4)*
1 tablespoon fish sauce

3 medium-sized bitter gourds
2 cups (16 fl oz) water
2 tablespoons sugar
3 tablespoons peanut oil
2 tablespoons Green Curry Paste *(page 4)*
1 cup (8 fl oz) coconut milk
1 cup (8 fl oz) water
1 teaspoon palm sugar
2 tablespoons fish sauce
3 kaffir lime leaves

1 **TO MAKE THE FILLING**, mix together all the ingredients.

2 Cut the bitter gourds into 2.5 cm (1 in) slices, discarding the tips and stem ends. With a small knife hollow out the centre membrane and seeds. Bring the water and sugar to the boil and blanch the slices, a few at a time, for 1–2 minutes. Drain.

3 Pack the pork mixture firmly into the gourd slices. Heat the oil and fry the gourd, a few slices at a time, to seal the pork and brown it slightly. Remove to a plate with a slotted spoon and pour off the oil, leaving only a tablespoon in the pan.

4 Fry the curry paste, stirring, until fragrant. Add the coconut milk, water, palm sugar, fish sauce and lime leaves, and stir until simmering. Gently slip the bitter gourd slices into the sauce and simmer for 20 minutes, or until the pork is cooked through. Serve with steamed jasmine rice.

# SWEET PORK

*Moo Wan* (Serves 6–8)

*Pork cooked until tender in a mixture of salty fish sauce and sweet palm sugar has quite an extraordinary flavour. The skin is shredded into fine, thread-like strips and included in salads, giving them another dimension and texture. The meat is cut up and fried in other dishes such as rice and noodles, but can also be sliced thinly and served, with chilli sauce, as an accompaniment to steamed jasmine rice.*

1 kg (2 lb) pork loin
½ cup palm sugar
½ cup (4 fl oz) fish sauce

1 Remove the rind from the pork and reserve. The pork may be cut into pieces or cooked whole, whichever you prefer.

2 Put the pork and rind into a saucepan with cold water to cover. Add the sugar and fish sauce, bring to the boil, skimming the top constantly of any scum. Lower the heat and simmer, covered, for about 1 hour.

3 After 1 hour, uncover and continue to cook until the pork is tender and the rind transparent. The rind should be soft enough to be pierced easily. Allow to cool in the liquid, then use as desired. The meat and liquid can be refrigerated for up to 1 week.

# STIR-FRIED CHILLI PORK WITH CASHEWS

## Moo Phad Mamuang Mimaparn *(Serves 4)*

*A quick dish to make, especially if you have ready-to-use curry paste.*

¼ cup raw cashews
½ cup (4 fl oz) peanut oil for
    frying
6 dried red chillies
500 g (1 lb) lean pork, sliced
    thinly
2 teaspoons Red Curry Paste
    *(page 3)* or *Tom Yum* Paste
    *(page 6)*
2 tablespoons fish sauce
2 tablespoons lime juice
1 teaspoon palm sugar
½ cup (4 fl oz) water
2 teaspoons Golden Mountain
    sauce *(page 209)*
1 teaspoon cornflour
    (cornstarch)
lettuce, carrot, cucumber and
    lime wedges (garnish)

1  Fry the cashews in the oil over medium heat, stirring constantly until golden brown. Lift out with a slotted spoon and drain on absorbent paper. Fry the dried chillies just until they turn dark and drain. Pour off all but 2 tablespoons of the oil.

2  On high heat fry the pork until it changes colour. Add the curry paste (or, for a more lemony flavour, use *tom yum* paste) and fry for a few minutes longer. Add the fish sauce, lime juice, sugar and water and simmer for 10 minutes. Add the Golden Mountain sauce to taste.

3  Thicken the sauce with cornflour mixed with a little cold water and turn off the heat before adding the fried cashews and chillies. Serve garnished with lettuce, slices of carrot and cucumber, and wedges of lime.

# SPICY PORK MINCE

*Phad Moo Sub* (Serves 4–6)

*This must be one of the quickest and tastiest ways with mince. In Thailand, pork mince (ground pork) would be used, but because most supermarkets and butchers sell a mixture of pork and veal mince, we have used this instead. The results are just as good.*

2 tablespoons peanut oil
1 tablespoon Pepper and
    Coriander Paste (*page 8*)
1 teaspoon finely chopped
    garlic
300 g (10 oz) minced (ground)
    pork and veal
1 teaspoon hot chilli sauce
1 teaspoon fish sauce
1 small onion, finely sliced
1 stem lemon grass, finely
    sliced

1 Heat a wok, add the oil and swirl to coat. Add the Pepper and Coriander Paste and the garlic and fry, stirring constantly, until fragrant.

2 Add the mince and continue to stir, breaking up any lumps, until the meat is no longer pink.

3 Mix in the chilli sauce and fish sauce. Cover with a lid, lower the heat and simmer for 15 minutes.

4 Stir in the onion and lemon grass and cook uncovered, stirring frequently, until the liquid reduces almost completely. Serve with steamed jasmine rice and a vegetable dish.

# MINCED PORK WITH BASIL

*Moo Sub Bai Krapow* *(Serves 4–6)*

1 cup (8 fl oz) coconut milk

3 teaspoons Pepper and
   Coriander Paste (*page 8*)

500 g (1 lb) lean minced
   (ground) pork

1 stem lemon grass, finely
   sliced

2 tablespoons Golden
   Mountain sauce (*page 209*)

20 basil leaves

2 red chillies, seeded and
   sliced

1  Heat ½ cup (4 fl oz) of the coconut milk, add the Pepper and Coriander Paste and cook until fragrant.

2  Stir in the pork mince and lemon grass and simmer until the pork is tender, stirring frequently and adding more coconut milk if required. The meat should be moist, not dry.

3  A few minutes before serving, stir in the Golden Mountain sauce, basil leaveas and red chillies. Serve with steamed jasmine rice.

*Red pork curry with young corn (page 105).*

*Stir-fried beef with broccoli and corn (page 124).*

# FRIED MEATBALLS

*Moo, Nuer Tod Mun* (Makes about 30 small balls)

*Serve these as an accompaniment to rice and curry, or simmer them in a curry sauce. The mixture may also be used to fill cucumber and zucchini (courgettes) that are simmered in soups (page 35).*

2 teaspoons finely chopped
  garlic
½ teaspoon salt
125 g (4 oz) minced (ground)
  beef
125 g (4 oz) minced (ground)
  pork
¼ teaspoon freshly ground
  black pepper
½ teaspoon grated nutmeg
2 tablespoons finely chopped
  fresh coriander
2 tablespoons finely chopped
  spring onions
2 teaspoons fish sauce
1 tablespoon beaten egg
plain (all-purpose) flour
peanut oil for frying

1 Sprinkle the garlic with the salt and crush to a smooth purée. Combine the garlic, beef and pork in a bowl with all the other ingredients except the flour and oil. Mix very well to distribute the flavours.

2 Take teaspoonfuls of the mixture and roll between wet hands to make small balls the size of marbles. Roll in flour and fry in hot oil over medium-low heat, shaking the pan frequently, until they are golden brown and cooked through. Drain on absorbent paper.

# EGGS FILLED WITH PORK AND SEAFOOD

*Kai Jah* (Serves 4–6)

4 eggs
½ cup chopped raw prawns
½ cup flaked cooked crab
    meat
½ cup chopped cooked pork
1 teaspoon Pepper and
    Coriander Paste (*page 8*)
1 tablespoon fish sauce or
    ½ teaspoon salt
1–2 tablespoons thick coconut
    milk
peanut oil for deep-frying

BATTER
½ cup (2 oz) plain (all-
    purpose) flour
2 tablespoons roasted rice
    flour (*page 208*)
½ cup (4 fl oz) lukewarm
    water
2 teaspoons peanut oil

1 Have the eggs at room temperature, not straight out of the refrigerator. Put them into a pan of cold water and slowly bring to the boil, stirring gently for the first 3 minutes so that the yolks are centred. Simmer for 8–10 minutes, then run cold water into the pan to cool the eggs quickly. Shell and cut the eggs in half lengthwise.

2 Scoop out the yolks and mash them with a fork. Add the rest of the ingredients except the oil and mix well.

3 Divide the mixture into 8 equal portions and fill the egg whites, moulding and smoothing the filling to look like a complete egg.

4 TO MAKE THE BATTER, whisk all the ingredients together until smooth, adding a little extra water if the batter is too thick.

5 Dip the eggs in the batter one at a time and fry in a deep saucepan until golden brown. Drain on absorbent paper and serve warm or cold, with Chilli Sauce (*page 54*) or Peanut Sauce (*page 56*) for dipping.

# PORK AND CRAB SAUSAGE

*Sai Klok Moo Gub Poo* (Serves 6)

*There are different types of sausages made and sold in Thailand and, depending on which region the recipe originated from they are either sour or hot or sweet . . . not totally, but those flavours predominate. Because the traditional way of cooking these sausages is over coals, they are ideal for barbecuing. When the sausage is nearly done, a handful of coconut from which the milk has been extracted is sprinkled over the fire to make fragrant smoke. Remember that when grating fresh coconut, not a bit of it is wasted. The shells make good firewood, and even after extracting three lots of milk, the used flesh can be packed into freezer bags and saved for the day when you want to sprinkle some over hot coals to give your Thai sausages that authentic flavour!*

sausage casing
250 g (8 oz) minced (ground)
    pork
125 g (4 oz) crab meat
1 tablespoon Red Curry Paste
    (*page 3*)
¼ cup roasted peanuts,
    coarsely chopped
¼ cup finely chopped purple
    shallots or spring onions
2 tablespoons finely chopped
    fresh coriander
2 teaspoons fish sauce
3 tablespoons thick coconut
    milk

1 Soak the sausage casing in a sink of cold water while making the filling. The reason I don't give a weight or measurement for this is because you are more or less at your butcher's mercy as you plead with him to part with some of his stock. He will grudgingly give you some and charge you whatever he thinks fit, but the sausages are worth it! There are thin and thick sausage casings; we used thin ones, but this is up to you.

2 Mix all the other ingredients together thoroughly, first making sure there are no bony bits in the crab meat.

3 Stretch one end of the sausage casing over the cold water tap and run water through. (It may be necessary to trim off any sections through which water spurts, otherwise the sausages will burst when they are filled.)

4 Tie a knot about 7 cm (3 in) from one end and secure with string. Using a funnel or a short length of plastic tube, push the filling into the casing with the handle of a wooden spoon or other object of suitable size. Coil the sausage as you go along. If preferred, twist at short intervals as in western-style sausages. A sausage-making machine will be very useful here.

5 Preheat a griller (broiler) and cook over glowing coals, placing the sausage as far away from the heat as possible so that it cooks thoroughly. Cooking time should be at least 25 minutes.

6 Sprinkle grated coconut on the coals during the last 10 minutes, or use soaked wood chips to impart a different flavour – hickory and mesquite are two of my favourites. Turn the sausage once during grilling. Slice thickly and serve with steamed jasmine rice.

# MINCED BEEF SALAD

*Larb* (Serves 4–6)

*There are two versions of Larb, one based on raw beef like Steak Tartare, while the other is lightly poached. Those who are not brave enough for raw steak may prefer the cooked version. If you wish to try the original, make sure the steak is very fresh, very lean and very finely minced.*

500 g (1 lb) lean grilling steak or premium quality minced (ground) steak
4 tablespoons lime juice
2 dried red chillies
3 tablespoons peanut oil
2 tablespoons roasted rice flour (*page 208*)
2 stems lemon grass, sliced
½ cup finely chopped purple onion or spring onion
½ cup chopped fresh mint leaves
2 tablespoons fish sauce or to taste
lettuce leaves, mint sprigs, lime wedges, fresh chilli slices (garnish)

---

**NOTE** *If you cannot find ready roasted and ground rice flour, it is worth making some – the flavour is essential to Larb. In a dry pan over medium heat put 3 tablespoons raw rice and shake the pan or stir constantly until the rice grains are toasty brown. Pound in a mortar and pestle.*

---

1 Ask the butcher to mince the steak for you. Mix in a bowl with the lime juice.

2 Fry the dried chillies in hot oil until they are almost black, about 2 minutes, and drain on absorbent paper. When cool they will be crisp and easy to chop finely, almost to a powder. Mix with the roasted rice powder.

3 Combine all the other ingredients apart from the garnish thoroughly. Arrange on lettuce leaves and garnish with mint sprigs, lime wedges and fresh chilli slices.

4 For the cooked version, poach the minced beef for a minute or two, only until the colour changes, in a small amount of boiling water. Drain (save the liquid for soup or a curry), mix in all the ingredients, garnish and serve.

# GREEN CURRY OF BEEF

*Kaeng Khiew Wan Nuer* (Serves 4–6)

*Like all curry dishes, this one gets better after a few days in the refrigerator. The recipe may be doubled successfully.*

750 g (1½ lb) lean round or
    blade steak
2 tablespoons peanut oil
3 tablespoons Green Curry
    Paste (*page 4*)
3 cups (24 fl oz) coconut milk
4 fresh, frozen or dried kaffir
    lime leaves, shredded
2 tablespoons fish sauce
2 fresh green chillies, finely
    chopped
1 teaspoon palm sugar
¼ cup chopped fresh
    coriander
¼ cup chopped fresh basil

1  Cut the beef into thick strips.

2  Heat the oil and fry the curry paste over medium heat until it is fragrant. Add the beef and stir-fry until it changes colour.

3  Add the coconut milk and stir until it comes to the boil, then lower the heat so it simmers. Add the lime leaves, fish sauce and chillies and cook uncovered over low heat for about 20 minutes, until the beef is tender.

4  Just before serving, stir in the sugar, coriander and basil. Serve with steamed jasmine rice.

# BEEF PANANG CURRY

*Panang Nuer* (Serves 4)

500 g (1 lb) round or blade
  steak
1 cup (8 fl oz) thick coconut
  milk
2–3 tablespoons Panang Curry
  Paste (*page 7*)
2 cups (16 fl oz) thin coconut
  milk
2 tablespoons fish sauce
4 fresh or dried kaffir lime
  leaves
2 red chillies, seeded and
  sliced
2 teaspoons palm sugar
2 tablespoons lime juice
½ cup roasted peanuts
¼ cup chopped fresh
  coriander
fresh basil leaves (optional)

1 Trim off any fat or sinew and cut the beef into slices, then into bite-sized pieces.

2 Heat half the thick coconut milk in a wok or saucepan and when it is oily, fry the Panang Curry Paste over medium heat, stirring, until it is fragrant.

3 Add the thin coconut milk, fish sauce, beef, lime leaves and chillies. Simmer until the beef is tender, adding more thin coconut milk if necessary.

4 Stir in the remaining thick coconut milk, palm sugar, lime juice and peanuts. Sprinkle with the fresh coriander and basil leaves and serve with steamed jasmine rice.

# MASAMAN BEEF CURRY

*Kaeng Masaman Nuer* (Serves 4)

*In this curry, you will taste the fragrant spices usually associated with Indian curries.*

500 g (1 lb) lean stewing beef
½ teaspoon salt
4 cardamom pods, bruised
2½ cups (20 fl oz) thin
   coconut milk
2 cups (16 fl oz) thick coconut
   milk
2–3 tablespoons Masaman
   Curry Paste (*page 5*)
10 small new potatoes,
   scrubbed
10 pickling onions, peeled
1 tablespoon fish sauce
3 tablespoons lime juice
2 teaspoons palm sugar
15–20 basil leaves
2 tablespoons crushed, roasted
   peanuts (optional)

1 Cut the beef into large cubes and put into a saucepan with the salt, cardamom pods and thin coconut milk. Simmer, uncovered, for about 1 hour until the meat is almost tender. Lift the meat from its cooking liquid with a slotted spoon. Reserve the stock for making soup.

2 Heat 1 cup (8 fl oz) of the thick coconut milk until oily, stir in the curry paste and fry until it smells fragrant.

3 Stir in the potatoes, onions and the meat. Simmer the meat and vegetables until tender, adding the remaining thick coconut milk as necessary. Stir in the fish sauce, lime juice, palm sugar and basil leaves. If preferred, sprinkle the curry with peanuts before serving.

# FRIED BEEF WITH BAMBOO SHOOTS AND MUSHROOMS

*Phad Nuer Normai, Hed (Serves 4)*

*This is typical of the way a small amount of meat can be stretched by adding vegetables and sufficiently strong flavours to make the whole dish tasty.*

*Canned bamboo shoots or straw mushrooms keep well in the refrigerator for about a week after opening, but change the water every day.*

250 g (8 oz) rump steak
1 tablespoon Pepper and
   Coriander Paste (*page 8*)
2 teaspoons finely chopped
   garlic
2 tablespoons peanut oil
¼ cup pea-sized eggplants
   (aubergines)
½ cup sliced bamboo shoot
½ cup drained straw
   mushrooms
2 red chillies, seeded and
   sliced
10 basil leaves
2 teaspoons fish sauce
1 teaspoon palm sugar
2 tender kaffir lime or citrus
   leaves, finely shredded

1  Trim off excess fat from the steak and cut the meat into thin strips. Marinate with half the Pepper and Coriander Paste for 1 hour.

2  Fry the garlic in the oil over medium heat, stirring, for a minute, taking care it does not brown. Add the remaining paste and fry until fragrant. Add the beef and stir-fry until it changes colour and is tender.

3  Add the eggplants, bamboo shoots and the mushrooms, which may be cut in half lengthwise so they absorb more flavour. Continue cooking until all the liquid is absorbed.

4  Stir in the chillies, basil leaves, fish sauce, palm sugar and lime leaves, heat through and serve with steamed jasmine rice or bean starch noodles.

# BEEF AND PUMPKIN CURRY

*Kaeng Nuer Fug Tong (Serves 6)*

*The sweetness of pumpkin goes well with the hot flavours of this curry.*

750 g (1½ lb) beef
750 g (1½ lb) pumpkin
2 tablespoons peanut oil
2–3 tablespoons Red Curry
   Paste (*page 3*)
2 cups (16 fl oz) thin coconut
   milk
3 kaffir lime leaves
2 or 3 large dried red chillies
5 or 6 fresh red chillies,
   seeded
2 tablespoons fish sauce
1 teaspoon palm sugar
½ cup (4 fl oz) thick coconut
   milk

1 Trim off any excess fat and cut the beef into cubes.

2 Peel the pumpkin and discard the membrane and seeds from the centre, then cut the pumpkin into cubes of the same size.

3 Heat the oil in a heavy saucepan or wok and fry the curry paste, stirring over medium heat until it is fragrant and oil shows around the edges.

4 Add the beef cubes and fry them in the mixture, stirring and turning them constantly until they change colour.

5 Add the thin coconut milk, lime leaves, chillies and fish sauce. Simmer for 30 minutes, then add the pumpkin and stir well. If necessary, add an extra cup (8 fl oz) of coconut milk so there is sufficient liquid to simmer the pumpkin. Continue to cook for a further 35–40 minutes until the pumpkin and beef are tender. Stir in the palm sugar until it dissolves and then the thick coconut milk. Serve the curry with steamed jasmine rice.

# BEEF AND SPINACH IN COCONUT MILK

*Kaeng Nuer Gub Pak Kom* (Serves 6)

1 bunch spinach, about 500 g
    (1 lb)
4 cups (32 fl oz) coconut milk
3 tablespoons Pepper and
    Coriander Paste (*page 8*)
2 stems lemon grass, finely
    sliced
1 tablespoon sliced fresh
    galangal or 3 slices bottled
    or dried galangal
2 tablespoons fish sauce
1 tablespoon palm sugar or
    brown sugar
500 g (1 lb) lean round steak,
    sliced into strips

1 Wash the spinach well and use only the leaves for this dish. Cut the leaves across twice.

2 In a wok stir the coconut milk and Pepper and Coriander Paste, lemon grass, galangal, fish sauce and sugar until simmering. Add the beef and cook gently, uncovered, for 20 minutes or until the beef is almost tender. Add the spinach and cook for about 8 minutes. Serve with steamed jasmine rice.

# STIR-FRIED BEEF WITH BROCCOLI AND CORN

*Phad Phed Nuer, Kao Poad Orn* (Serves 4)

250 g (8 oz) round steak,
    sliced into strips
2 cups (16 fl oz) coconut milk
2 kaffir lime leaves
2 tablespoons peanut oil
2 tablespoons Red Curry Paste
    (*page 3*)
2 cups broccoli florets
1 cup young corn cobs
¾ cup (6 fl oz) coconut milk
4 spring onions, sliced
1 tablespoon fish sauce
1 teaspoon palm sugar
coriander leaves (garnish)

1 Cook the beef until tender in the coconut milk with the lime leaves. Drain, reserving the liquid.

2 Heat the oil and cook the curry paste until fragrant. Add the beef, broccoli and corn and cook for 3 to 4 minutes, stirring constantly.

3 Add the coconut milk and cook over moderately high heat until it is all absorbed and the meat and vegetables are tender. Add some of the reserved cooking liquid if necessary.

4 Stir in the spring onions, fish sauce and palm sugar and garnish with coriander leaves. Serve with steamed jasmine rice.

# MINCED BEEF WITH DRIED SHRIMP

*Phad Nuer Sub Goong Haeng* (Serves 4–6)

½ cup dried shrimp
2 tablespoons peanut oil
1 onion, finely chopped
2 tablespoons Pepper and
 Coriander Paste (*page 8*)
500 g (1 lb) minced (ground)
 steak
2 teaspoons palm sugar
2–3 tablespoons fish sauce
2 red chillies, seeded and
 sliced
3 tablespoons soaked wood
 fungus, sliced
¼ cup fresh mint leaves
¼ cup fresh basil leaves

1 Soak the shrimp in hot water for 10 minutes or until softened.

2 Heat the oil in a wok and fry the onion, stirring frequently, until soft and golden.

3 Add the Pepper and Coriander Paste and fry, stirring, for 3 minutes or until fragrant. Add the minced steak and the drained prawns and stir-fry until the beef is no longer pink.

4 Cover and simmer until the liquid that comes out of the beef is almost all absorbed and the beef is tender.

5 Stir in the palm sugar, fish sauce, chillies and wood fungus. Add the fresh mint and basil leaves (which should be roughly chopped if large) and toss together for a minute or two before serving with steamed jasmine rice. When served cold it makes a nice addition to a mixed salad.

# SWEET AND HOT CRISP BEEF

*Nuer Khem Phad* *(Serves 4–6)*

*This side dish is usually served with Iced Rice (page 171) but is just as delicious with rice. The oil in which the beef is fried is full of flavour and is delicious when sparingly mixed with steamed jasmine rice.*

500 g corned (salted) silverside
3 tablespoons peanut oil
1 teaspoon crushed garlic
1 teaspoon chilli powder
1 tablespoon palm sugar
1 tablespoon fish sauce
crisp-fried onion and garlic
    flakes (*page 208*) (optional)

1 Put the corned beef in a saucepan with cold water to cover and bring to the boil. Lower the heat and simmer, covered, for 1 hour or until the beef is very tender. Drain well and leave until cool enough to handle. Lift the meat onto a board and gently tease the fibres loose with a fork. Discard any fat or gristle.

2 Heat the oil in a wok and fry the beef, stirring constantly for 3 or 4 minutes or until it is slightly brown and crisp. Add the garlic and chilli powder, and continue tossing for a further minute or until the garlic smells fragrant.

3 Stir in the palm sugar and fish sauce. As the palm sugar melts it will coat the beef. Pour the beef and the oil, flavoured with garlic and chilli, onto a serving dish. If desired, sprinkle the beef with crisp-fried onion and garlic flakes.

# FISH AND OTHER SEAFOOD

Next to rice, fish is the most important item in the Thai diet because of the bountiful harvest of the sea, rivers, flooded paddy fields and canals that are so much a part of Thailand.

Live prawns (shrimp), crabs and crayfish, squid, mussels and dozens of different kinds of fish are plentiful in Thai markets.

Salted dried seafood is sold in another section of the markets, and this is also important in the diet – not so much as a main ingredient, but as a flavouring. If garlic, coriander, pepper and chillies are important flavours in Thai cooking, so are flavourings derived from fish and other seafood. There is fish sauce, the ubiquitous *nam pla*, found in most recipes and placed on the table as a condiment. Almost equally prominent is dried shrimp paste, or *kapi*, which is used to spark up the flavour of most dishes, including those featuring meat. Small dried shrimp are also indispensable.

Don't let the unfamiliarity of the combination stop you trying the recipes – the flavours blend wonderfully.

# FRIED PRAWN BALLS

*Look Chin Goong Tod* (Makes 12–16)

*Serve as an accompaniment to rice and curries, or as an appetiser or party savoury. Rice powder can be bought from Asian food stores, or see page 118 for instructions on how to make your own.*

185 g (6 oz) raw prawn
(shrimp) meat
2 spring onions, finely
chopped
1 teaspoon Pepper and
Coriander Paste (*page 8*)
1 teaspoon cornflour
(cornstarch)
1 teaspoon fish sauce
¼ cup roasted rice powder or
dried breadcrumbs
peanut oil for frying

1 Remove any veins from the prawns and chop the prawns finely.

2 Mix in the rest of the ingredients except the rice powder and oil. Form into marble-sized balls and roll in rice powder or breadcrumbs to coat.

3 Heat the oil in a wok or frying pan and fry a few balls at a time until golden. They will not need long cooking. Drain on absorbent paper and serve warm.

# FISH WITH COCONUT CREAM SAUCE

*Pla Ob Kati* (Serves 2)

2 fillets or cutlets of your
  choice of fish, cooked
½ cup (4 fl oz) coconut milk
2 teaspoons rice flour
¼ teaspoon salt
1 tablespoon lime or lemon
  juice
2 teaspoons fish sauce
red chilli, seeded and sliced
  (garnish)
spring onions, finely sliced
  (garnish)
fresh coriander, chopped
  (garnish)

1 The fish may be steamed, grilled (broiled), microwaved or fried, whichever method is most convenient. Cook it until just done, don't overcook.

2 In a small pan over low heat stir the coconut milk, rice flour and salt until it thickens.

3 Sprinkle the fish with the lime or lemon juice and fish sauce, and spoon over the coconut milk mixture. Garnish with chillies, spring onions and coriander.

# POMFRET WITH COCONUT

*Pla Lard Kati* (Serves 2)

1 pomfret (or other delicate
   flat fish), approximately
   500 g (1 lb)
1 tablespoon peanut oil
1½ tablespoons Green Curry
   Paste (*page 4*)
1 teaspoon lime juice
½ cup grated fresh coconut
2 tablespoons finely sliced
   spring onions
2 tablespoons chopped fresh
   coriander
¾ cup (6 fl oz) coconut milk
1 teaspoon fish sauce
1 small green chilli, chopped
cornflour (cornstarch)
peanut oil for frying

1 Have the fish cleaned and scaled if necessary. Lightly score the flesh where it is thickest.

2 Heat the oil and fry the curry paste, stirring, until it is fragrant. Take 1 teaspoon of the fried paste and mix it with the lime juice and half the grated coconut. Pack into the cavity of the fish.

3 Add the remaining coconut, spring onions, coriander, coconut milk, fish sauce and green chilli to the fried curry paste and simmer, stirring, for 5 minutes. Cool slightly, then purée in a blender at high speed.

4 Dust the fish with cornflour to coat. Heat the oil for shallow-frying and fry the fish, first on one side and then the other, until golden brown. Transfer to a serving plate and spoon the sauce over to coat. Serve the remaining sauce in a separate bowl.

*Stuffed fried crab (page 145).*

*Red curry of prawns (page 139).*

# FISH IN CHILLI-TOMATO SAUCE

*Pla Saus Makua Tet (Serves 4)*

500 g (1 lb) fish fillets
2 tablespoons vinegar
2 tablespoons fish sauce
2 tablespoons hot chilli sauce
1 tablespoon palm sugar
3 tablespoons peanut oil
2 onions, finely chopped
3 red tomatoes, peeled, seeded
    and chopped
fresh coriander, roughly
    chopped (garnish)
red chillies, finely sliced
    (garnish)

---

**NOTE** *To peel tomatoes, drop them into boiling water for 30 seconds. Lift out with a slotted spoon and drop into cold water. Peel. Halve the tomatoes and gently squeeze out the seeds, then chop the shells roughly.*

---

**1** Rinse and dry the fish. In a small bowl mix together the vinegar, fish sauce, chilli sauce and palm sugar, stirring to dissolve the sugar.

**2** Heat the oil and fry the onions over moderate heat, stirring frequently, until it is soft and starts to turn golden. Add the tomatoes and the vinegar mixture, cover and simmer for 15–20 minutes, until the sauce is thick.

**3** Add the fish fillets, spooning the sauce over them. Cover and cook gently until the fish is done. Garnish with coriander and red chillies. Serve with steamed jasmine rice.

# WHOLE FRIED FISH WITH MUSHROOM AND GINGER SAUCE

*Platod Lard Khing Hedhom* (Serves 4)

*The sauce may be prepared beforehand and reheated just before serving, while the fish is being cooked. A delicate white fish such as flounder, pomfret or snapper is best.*

4 dried shiitake mushrooms
¼ cup (2 fl oz) vinegar
2 tablespoons sugar
⅓ cup (2½ fl oz) water
1 tablespoon light soy sauce
2 teaspoons cornflour
  (cornstarch)
2 tablespoons finely sliced
  spring onions
2 tablespoons sweet red
  ginger, shredded
1 whole fish, about 750 g
  (1½ lb)
salt
plain (all-purpose) flour
peanut oil for frying

1 Pour boiling water over the mushrooms, cover and leave to soak and soften for 30 minutes. Discard the stems and slice the caps finely.

2 In a stainless steel saucepan combine the sliced mushrooms, vinegar, sugar, water and soy sauce and simmer for 5 minutes.

3 Dissolve the cornflour in 1 tablespoon of cold water. Add the spring onions to the saucepan, then stir in the cornflour. Keep stirring over medium heat until the sauce boils and thickens. If preparing ahead, do not add the ginger until ready to serve or it will lose some of its pretty colour. Stir in only just before spooning it over the fish.

4 Wash the fish thoroughly and scrub the cavity with damp absorbent paper dipped in salt. If the fish has thick flesh, score it diagonally halfway to the bone to allow heat to penetrate. Dip the fish in flour and dust off the excess.

5 Heat the oil in a wok or frying pan until smoking and gently slide in the fish. Fry, ladling oil over the top of the fish, for about 5 minutes. Carefully turn the fish over and fry the other side. Drain on absorbent paper, then slide the fish onto a serving dish. Spoon over some of the sauce and serve the rest in a bowl. Serve immediately.

# FISH BALL CURRY WITH VEGETABLES

*Kaeng Phed Look Chin Pla, Pak* (Serves 4)

500 g (1 lb) fish fillets
1½ teaspoons cornflour
  (cornstarch)
1 teaspoon Pepper and
  Coriander Paste (*page 8*)
250 g (8 oz) green beans or
  zucchini (courgettes)
1½ cups (12 fl oz) thin
  coconut milk
2 tablespoons Red Curry Paste
  (*page 3*)
¼ cup chopped spring onions
½ cup (4 fl oz) thick coconut
  milk
1–2 teaspoons palm sugar
1 tablespoon lime juice
chilli, sliced (garnish)
fresh coriander (garnish)

1  Remove all skin and any bones remaining in the fish fillets. Chop the fish finely or blend to a paste in a food processor, adding the cornflour and Pepper and Coriander Paste. Shape teaspoonfuls of the fish mixture into balls. Place on a plate lined with greaseproof paper.

2  Top and tail the beans, string them and slice thinly. If using zucchini, cut into julienne.

3  Heat ¾ cup (6 fl oz) of the coconut milk until it separates, add the Red Curry Paste and cook, stirring, until fragrant. Add the remaining coconut milk, stirring gently, until boiling.

4  Add the beans and simmer for 5 minutes. Add the fish balls and when they come back to a boil, reduce the heat and simmer for 3 minutes longer. Shake the pan gently from time to time to prevent sticking. Stir in the spring onions, thick coconut milk, palm sugar and lime juice. Simmer 1 minute more. Garnish with chilli and coriander.

# FRIED FISH WITH TAMARIND SAUCE

*Pla Jian (Serves 4)*

*Use this piquant sauce on whole fish, fillets or cutlets. It stands up well to any strongly flavoured fish.*

1 kg (2 lb) fish
1 teaspoon salt
1 teaspoon ground turmeric
½ teaspoon pepper
peanut oil for shallow-frying
1½ teaspoons crushed garlic
2 tablespoons light soy sauce
2 tablespoons fish sauce
¼ cup (2 fl oz) tamarind
   liquid (*page 212*)
1 tablespoon palm sugar
1 or 2 fresh red chillies, sliced
3 tablespoons sliced spring
   onions
fresh coriander (garnish)

1 Wash and dry the fish thoroughly and rub over the salt, turmeric and pepper.

2 Heat the oil and fry the fish on medium heat until golden on both sides. Drain on absorbent paper.

3 Pour away all but 1 tablespoon of oil and fry the garlic over low heat, stirring, until it is pale golden. Add the sauces, tamarind liquid and sugar mixed together. When boiling, add the fish and simmer over medium heat for a few minutes until the sauce thickens slightly.

4 Add the chillies and spring onions, simmer 1 minute more, and serve garnished with coriander leaves.

# STEAMED FISH WITH TAMARIND AND GINGER

*Planung Khing* (Serves 4)

*While there are many recipes for fried fish with tamarind, if you buy a delicate white fish try cooking it in steam rather than oil. The piquant sauce with tamarind makes it a tasty dish.*

1 medium or 2 small whole
   fish
coarse salt
1 teaspoon finely grated fresh
   ginger
½ teaspoon salt

SAUCE
1 tablespoon peanut oil
1 teaspoon finely chopped
   garlic
1 tablespoon shredded ginger
4 spring onions, finely sliced
1 teaspoon palm sugar
1 tablespoon tamarind pulp
   concentrate or lime juice
1 tablespoon fish sauce
¼ cup (2 fl oz) water
1 teaspoon cornflour
   (cornstarch)
fresh coriander leaves
   (garnish)
red chilli strips (garnish)

1  Have the fish cleaned and scaled. Dip paper towels in coarse salt and scrub inside the cavity to get rid of any blood. Rinse and blot dry. Score the fish from head to tail three or four times, depending on the size of the fish. Rub inside and out with the grated ginger and salt.

2  Place the fish in a lightly oiled heatproof dish and steam over boiling water until it is done, about 10 minutes. The flesh should be opaque when tested at the thickest part. Carefully remove to a plate and keep warm while making the sauce.

3  **TO MAKE THE SAUCE,** heat the oil and on a low heat fry the garlic for a few seconds. Add the ginger shreds and spring onions and cook for a few seconds until they are soft.

4  Add the sugar, tamarind pulp or lime juice, fish sauce and water. Bring to the boil, and stir in the cornflour mixed with a tablespoon of cold water. As soon as the mixture clears and thickens, spoon over the fish. Garnish with fresh coriander and chilli, and serve with steamed jasmine rice.

# HOT AND SOUR PRAWNS WITH CUCUMBER

*Goong Lon Tang-Gwa* (Serves 6)

1½ cups (12 fl oz) coconut milk

2 tablespoons Red Curry Paste (*page 3*)

750 g (1½ lb) prawns (shrimp), shelled and deveined

1 large green cucumber, peeled, seeded and sliced

2 teaspoons dried tamarind pulp

½ cup (4 fl oz) hot water

2 tablespoons fish sauce

1 tablespoon palm sugar

2 or 3 red chillies, seeded and finely sliced

1 tablespoon lime juice

1 Heat about ½ cup (4 fl oz) of the thick top portion of the coconut milk until oil shows around the edges.

2 Add the Red Curry Paste and stir over medium heat until fragrant. Stir in the remaining coconut milk and bring to a boil.

3 Add the prawns and cucumber, return to the boil and cook for 2 minutes.

4 Soak the tamarind pulp in hot water, dissolve and strain. Mix the tamarind liquid, fish sauce, palm sugar, chillies and lime juice into the prawns. Once the mixture comes to the boil, whisk off the heat. Serve with steamed jasmine rice or noodles.

# RED CURRY OF PRAWNS

*Kaeng Phed Goong (Serves 6)*

*For the best flavour, cook and serve the prawns in their shells. If you follow my directions on how to prepare them, it will be easy to remove the shell with a spoon and fork. See colour plate on page 132.*

750 g (1½ lb) large raw
    prawns (jumbo shrimp)
1 cup (8 fl oz) thick coconut
    milk
2–3 tablespoons Red Curry
    Paste (*page 3*)
2 cups (16 fl oz) thin coconut
    milk
4 kaffir lime leaves
½ teaspoon finely grated lime
    rind
2 tablespoons fish sauce
2 teaspoons palm sugar

1 With a pair of kitchen scissors trim each prawn's long feelers and cut open the shell down the curve of the back but do not remove it. With a sharp, pointed knife slit the flesh to expose the vein and lift it out. Rinse and drain the cleaned prawns.

2 In a wok or frying pan, heat the thick coconut milk until bubbling, add the Red Curry Paste and cook, stirring, until oily and fragrant.

3 Add the thin coconut milk, lime leaves and rind, fish sauce and palm sugar. Bring to a boil, then add the prawns and simmer uncovered, stirring now and then, for 15 minutes, or until the prawns are cooked and the sauce has slightly reduced and thickened. Serve with steamed jasmine rice and a cucumber or cabbage salad.

# GREEN CURRY OF PRAWNS

*Kaeng Khiew Wan Goong (Serves 4)*

2 cups (16 fl oz) thick coconut
    milk
2 tablespoons Green Curry
    Paste (*page 4*)
375 g (12 oz) king prawns
    (jumbo shrimp), shelled
    and deveined
2 tablespoons fish sauce
2 teaspoons sugar
½ teaspoon grated kaffir lime
    rind or 3 kaffir lime leaves,
    shredded

1 In a wok bring 1 cup (8 fl oz) of the coconut milk to the boil and stir until oily.

2 Add the Green Curry Paste and stir until cooked and fragrant.

3 Stir in the prawns and remaining coconut milk and simmer 5 minutes longer. Add the fish sauce, sugar and lime rind, and adjust the seasoning if necessary. Once the sauce has reduced slightly and thickened, whisk off the heat. Serve with steamed jasmine rice.

# CHILLI PRAWN WITH SHREDDED LIME LEAF

*Phat Prik Goong Bai Makrut (Serves 4–6)*

*As in other Thai recipes, the lime leaf referred to is kaffir lime (citrus hystrix). While the dried leaves may be simmered in curries and soups, where used as a feature of the dish as in this recipe, they must be fresh. If you haven't a source of fresh kaffir lime leaves, don't despair. I have used other varieties of young citrus leaves from my garden and while they don't have quite the same fragrance, they still add a certain magic to the dish when bitten into.*

500 g (1 lb) medium-sized raw
   prawns (shrimp)
2 teaspoons finely chopped
   fresh ginger
1 tablespoon fish sauce
1 teaspoon sugar
½ cup sliced spring onions
4–6 dried red chillies, seeded
2 teaspoons finely chopped
   fresh or bottled galangal
1 tablespoon chopped lemon
   grass
½ teaspoon finely grated
   kaffir lime rind
½ teaspoon black peppercorns
4 cloves garlic
2 coriander roots or 6 stalks,
   chopped
1 small onion, finely chopped
2 tablespoons peanut oil
¾ cup (6 fl oz) thick coconut
   milk
1 teaspoon rice flour
½ teaspoon salt
lime leaves, finely shredded
   (garnish)
chilli, finely shredded
   (garnish)

1 Shell the prawns, leaving just the last segment of shell and the tail. Devein carefully, and with a sharp knife slit each prawn in half from the top, for about a third of its length.

2 Combine the ginger, fish sauce, sugar and spring onions with the prawns and set aside to marinate for about 10 minutes.

3 Soak the chillies in hot water for 10 minutes then drain. Pound together the chillies, galangal, lemon grass, lime rind, peppercorns, garlic, coriander and onion to form a paste.

4 Heat a wok or frying pan, add the oil and stir-fry the pounded ingredients until fragrant. Add the marinated prawns and cook until they change colour, turning constantly, about 3 minutes. Remove from the heat.

5 Heat the coconut milk in a small saucepan, reserving 2 tablespoons for mixing with the rice flour and salt. Stir the rice flour mixture into the coconut milk as it comes to the boil and continue stirring until it thickens. Pour immediately into the centre of a serving plate. Place the prawns on the sauce and sprinkle over the lime leaf and fresh chilli.

# GIANT STUFFED PRAWNS

*Goong Sod Sai (Serves 4)*

*Sometimes it is possible to buy the giant prawns that are so popular in Thailand. But the recipe adapts just as well to local king prawns. This lovely sauce can be made ahead and reheated.*

**SAUCE**
**3 dried chillies, seeded**
**¼ cup dried shrimp**
**1 teaspoon chopped garlic**
**½ cup (4 fl oz) thick coconut milk**
**2 teaspoons palm sugar**
**1 tablespoon fish sauce**
**1 tablespoon lime juice**
**1 teaspoon tamarind pulp concentrate**
**½ cup thin coconut milk**

**5 large prawns (jumbo shrimp)**
**1 tablespoon finely chopped spring onions**
**½ teaspoon Pepper and Coriander Paste (*page 8*)**
**⅛ teaspoon salt**
**2 or 3 kaffir lime leaves, finely shredded (garnish)**
**1 red chilli, finely shredded (garnish)**

**1 TO MAKE THE SAUCE,** break the dried chillies into pieces and soak in a little boiling water for 10 minutes until softened. Soak the dried shrimp in just enough hot water to cover for 10 minutes.

**2** Put the drained chillies, shrimp and garlic in an electric blender and grind everything finely, adding a little coconut milk if necessary to facilitate blending; or pound in a mortar and pestle.

**3** Heat the coconut milk until oily and add the blended mixture. Cook for a few minutes, stirring well. Stir in the palm sugar, fish sauce, lime juice and tamarind liquid. Gradually stir in the thin coconut milk and simmer to reduce and thicken the sauce.

**4** Wash the prawns and split the shells down the back. Remove the vein from each prawn and with a sharp knife slit four of the prawns halfway through.

**5** Remove the fifth prawn from its shell and chop finely. Mix the prawn meat with the spring onions, Pepper and Coriander Paste, and salt. Divide into four equal portions and stuff into the split in each prawn.

**6** Place the prawns in a steamer and steam over boiling water for 15–20 minutes, or until the shells turn red. (The legs take longer to change colour and in this time the prawns could be overcooked. Since the legs are too fine to yield meat, remove the steamer from the heat once the prawns are cooked.) Arrange on a plate and spoon over the sauce. Garnish with shreds of lime leaf and chilli, and serve with steamed jasmine rice.

# CURRY OF CRAB CLAWS AND PRAWN BALLS

## *Kaeng Phed Gampoo, Look Chin Goong* (Serves 4–6)

*This is a variation on Red Curry of Crab (page 143), but easier to eat because you don't have to ferret out the meat from within the crab shells. Ready-shelled claws may be bought, usually by the box, from a good fish shop. Store them in the freezer and thaw as required.*

250 g (8 oz) minced (ground) pork
375 g (12 oz) raw prawns (shrimp), shelled, deveined and chopped
1 tablespoon Pepper and Coriander Paste (*page 8*)
1 tablespoon fish sauce
1 or 2 small red chillies, seeded and chopped
2 tablespoons finely chopped spring onions
Curry Sauce (*page 143*)
12 crab claws

1 Combine the pork mince with the prawns, Pepper and Coriander Paste, fish sauce, chillies and spring onions. Form into small balls.

2 Prepare the Curry Sauce according to page 143. When the gravy has simmered for 10 minutes, add the balls and simmer until firm, shaking the pan rather than stirring so they don't break up. Cook for 5 minutes, then add the crab claws, gently slipping them into the sauce so they will absorb as much flavour as possible. Simmer for a further 10–15 minutes, and serve with steamed jasmine rice.

# RED CURRY OF CRAB

*Kaeng Phed Poo* (Serves 4–6)

*This is such a superb dish that when we eat it at home, it is the only dish on the menu, served with steaming hot jasmine rice. One needs to concentrate on picking the sweet flesh from the crabs, and other dishes would only be a distraction.*

4 medium to large live crabs

CURRY SAUCE
2–3 tablespoons Red Curry
    Paste (*page 3*)
1 teaspoon finely grated kaffir
    lime rind
½ cup chopped small purple
    shallots
1 cup (8 fl oz) thick coconut
    milk
6 kaffir lime leaves
3 tablespoons finely sliced
    lemon grass
2 or 3 green chillies, seeded
    and sliced
2½ cups (20 fl oz) coconut
    milk
1 tablespoon fish sauce
1 tablespoon palm sugar
2 tablespoons lime juice

1 Either put the crabs in the freezer for several hours, or boil them just long enough for the shells to turn red – there seems to be no agreement on which is the more humane method of dispatching them. Remove the top shells and clean the crabs, discarding the feathery tissue under the carapace. Break the bodies in half and crack the large claws so flavours can penetrate.

2 **TO MAKE THE CURRY SAUCE**, combine the curry paste with the lime rind (use any available limes if kaffir limes prove elusive) and the shallots.

3 Heat the thick coconut milk in a wok or frying pan and cook, stirring, until oily. Add the curry paste mixture and stir over medium heat until it smells fragrant.

4 Add the lime leaves, lemon grass, chillies and the coconut milk. Stir while bringing it to simmering point. Add the crabs and simmer for 15–20 minutes, or until the crabs are cooked.

5 Stir in the fish sauce, palm sugar and lime juice and cook a few minutes longer, adding a little hot water if the sauce has reduced too much. Serve with steamed jasmine rice.

# CRAB CLAWS WITH CHILLI SAUCE

*Gampoo Yudsai Lard Prik* (Serves 4–6)

1 teaspoon chopped coriander
   roots
5 whole black peppercorns
1 tablespoon finely chopped
   lemon grass
150 g (5 oz) raw prawn
   (shrimp) meat, finely
   chopped
150 g (5 oz) minced (ground)
   pork
2 tablespoons finely chopped
   fresh coriander
½ teaspoon salt
12 crab claws

SAUCE
2 tablespoons sweet hot chilli
   sauce
2 teaspoons fish sauce
2 tablespoons lime juice
2 teaspoons palm sugar or
   1½ tablespoons sugar
4 tablespoons water
2 teaspoons cornflour
   (cornstarch) or arrowroot
kaffir lime leaf (garnish)
lettuce (garnish)

1 Pound the coriander roots, peppercorns and lemon grass to a fine paste. Mix with the prawn meat and pork. Add the coriander and salt and mix well. Divide into 12 equal portions and mould around the flesh of the crab claws. Steam over boiling water for 10–12 minutes, until the shells turn red and the filling is cooked.

2 TO MAKE THE SAUCE, place all the ingredients except the cornflour and garnishes in a small pan and cook, stirring, until boiling. Mix the cornflour with a little cold water, stir into the sauce until it thickens and spoon over the crab claws. Garnish with shreds of kaffir lime leaf and serve on a bed of curly lettuce.

# STUFFED FRIED CRAB

*Poo Cha* (Serves 4)

*If you have some Pepper and Coriander Paste to hand, substitute the black pepper and coriander with 2 teaspoons of the paste. See colour plate on page 131.*

4 blue swimmer crabs, cooked
250 g (8 oz) raw prawns
   (shrimp)
½ cup soaked bean starch
   vermicelli, cut into 2.5 cm
   (1 in) lengths
250 g (8 oz) minced (ground)
   pork
2 tablespoons finely chopped
   spring onions
1 clove garlic
½ teaspoon salt
1 egg
1 tablespoon cornflour
   (cornstarch)
¼ teaspoon ground black
   pepper
2 tablespoons chopped fresh
   coriander
½ teaspoon finely chopped
   red chilli
3 cups (24 fl oz) peanut oil for
   frying
chilli flowers (garnish)
fresh coriander (garnish)

1 Carefully remove the top shell or carapace from the crabs and discard the feathery grey tissue underneath. Wash and dry the top shells. Break open the bodies and claws and remove the crab meat.

2 Shell and devein the prawns and chop finely. Put the prawns and vermicelli into a bowl with the pork, spring onions and crab meat.

3 Crush the garlic with the salt. Beat the egg and mix in the cornflour, crushed garlic, pepper, coriander and chilli. Add to the ingredients in the bowl and mix thoroughly. Fill the crab shells with the seasoned mixture.

4 Heat the oil in a wok or frying pan and fry the crabs, ladling oil over the top. Fry on medium heat for 7 or 8 minutes, so the filling cooks through by the time it is golden brown on the surface. Drain on absorbent paper, arrange on a serving plate and garnish with chilli flowers and sprigs of fresh coriander.

# STUFFED CURRIED MUSSELS

*Hor Mok Mang Poo* (Serves 4)

*Filled with a spicy pork mixture and simmered in a curry sauce, these mussels are delicious when served with rice.*

500 g (1 lb) small mussels
125 g (4 oz) minced (ground) pork
2 teaspoons Pepper and Coriander Paste (*page 8*) or Red Curry Paste (*page 3*)
1 tablespoon finely chopped lemon grass or zest of 1 lemon
½ teaspoon grated kaffir lime rind
2 tablespoons thinly sliced spring onions
2 teaspoons cornflour (cornstarch)
2 teaspoons fish sauce
1 teaspoon palm sugar
1 egg white

CURRY SAUCE
1½ cups (12 fl oz) coconut milk
2 tablespoons Green Curry Paste (*page 4*)
2 or 3 kaffir lime leaves
2 tablespoons fish sauce
1 tablespoon lime juice
1 red chilli, seeded and sliced
2 spring onions, chopped

1 Scrub the mussels well with a brush under cold water. Beard them by giving a sharp tug at the brown fibres protruding from the shell. The shells should be tightly shut – discard any which are not. Place the mussels on a rack and steam until the shells just open. Discard any which remain closed. Remove each top shell and discard.

2 Combine the pork and the rest of the ingredients, mixing well. Top each mussel with a heaped teaspoon of the mixture, smoothing it neatly into the shell.

3 **TO MAKE THE CURRY SAUCE**, heat about ½ cup of the rich top portion of the coconut milk until oil appears around the edges. Add the curry paste and cook, stirring, for a few minutes until fragrant.

4 Add the rest of the coconut milk, lime leaves and fish sauce and stir until simmering. On a low heat cook the mussels in this sauce for 10 minutes or until the filling is firm. Add the lime juice, red chilli and spring onions and simmer for a minute longer.

# VEGETABLES

The markets in Thailand were a real eye-opener. There were mushrooms I had never seen before and others which hitherto I had found only in cans. Also in profusion were fresh bamboo shoots still wearing their fuzzy wrappings; tender green asparagus in huge bunches; green pawpaws; gourds of many shapes and sizes and pendulous purple banana flowers which are used as a vegetable. Wing beans, snake beans, okra, sataw beans, chillies of all shapes, sizes and colours were everywhere, as well as small bunches of herbs and flavourings I can only describe as a Thai 'bouquet garni' . . . stems of lemon grass, slices of fresh turmeric and galangal, basil, coriander, and kaffir lime leaves.

To the vegetable vendors, it seemed not at all incongruous that mundane vegetables sat side by side with large piles of exotic, dew-fresh orchids. In any florist's shop in the West a few bunches of the same flowers would command a price high enough to purchase the Thai vendor's entire stock!

# MIXED VEGETABLES IN COCONUT MILK

*Tom Kati Pak Ruam* *(Serves 4–6)*

*For this recipe, any fresh vegetable in season may be combined; cut them into pieces of similar size. Fresh asparagus is very popular in Thailand, so use it when available. Pumpkin, zucchini (courgettes), young corn cobs, celery, beans, water chestnuts, bamboo shoots, and dried mushrooms that have been soaked and sliced are just some suggestions.*

300 g (10 oz) mixed vegetables
2 cloves garlic
2 or 3 red chillies, sliced
1 stem lemon grass, finely
    sliced or 2 strips lemon zest
2 kaffir lime leaves or
    ½ teaspoon grated kaffir
    lime rind
1 cup (8 fl oz) coconut milk
1 tablespoon fish sauce
1 tablespoon lime juice
10 fresh basil leaves

1 Prepare the vegetables by washing, peeling where necessary and cutting them into bite-sized pieces.

2 Pound the garlic, chillies, lemon grass and lime rind to a paste. (If using lime leaves, simmer them whole with the vegetables and coconut milk.)

3 Heat half the coconut milk until oily and fry the paste until fragrant. Add the prepared vegetables and remaining coconut milk with a little water if necessary. Simmer for 5 minutes, or until the vegetables are tender but crisp. Stir in the fish sauce, lime juice and basil leaves and serve with steamed jasmine rice or noodles.

# BANANA CAPSICUM CURRY

*Kaeng Prik Yuak Sod Sai* (Serves 4)

*Banana capsicums are an ideal size for filling with savoury mixtures, and their flavour is distinctive without being pungent.*

4 medium-sized banana
   capsicums (bell peppers)
125 g (4 oz) minced (ground)
   pork
60 g (2 oz) raw prawns
   (shrimp), chopped
1 teaspoon garlic, finely
   chopped
1 teaspoon Pepper and
   Coriander Paste (*page 8*)
1¼ cups (10 fl oz) coconut
   milk
2 tablespoons Red Curry Paste
   (*page 3*)
2 teaspoons palm sugar
1 tablespoon fish sauce
1 teaspoon paprika
2 or 3 lime leaves
½ cup basil leaves
2 red chillies, seeded and
   sliced

1 Cut the tops off the capsicums and remove the seeds and pith. Combine the pork, prawns, garlic, and Pepper and Coriander Paste, and pack into the capsicums with a teaspoon.

2 Heat half the coconut milk and cook the curry paste until fragrant. Stir in the remaining coconut milk, sugar, fish sauce, paprika and lime leaves. Place the capsicums in the simmering sauce and cook for 20–25 minutes, or until tender, turning after 10–15 minutes. Place them on a plate and stir the basil leaves and chillies into the sauce before pouring over the capsicums.

# BEAN CURD IN CABBAGE ROLLS

*Kalum Plee Pan Tao Hu* (Makes 6 rolls)

400 g (13 oz) soft bean curd
6 green cabbage leaves
6 spring onion tops
1 tablespoon peanut oil
250 g (8 oz) minced (ground)
   beef
2 tablespoons fish sauce
2 tablespoons palm sugar
1 teaspoon Pepper and
   Coriander Paste (*page 8*)
¼ cup chopped garlic chives
   or spring onions
1 egg, beaten
1 cup (8 fl oz) stock (*page 34*)
2 tablespoons Golden
   Mountain sauce (*page 209*)
2 teaspoons rice flour
2 tablespoons lime juice
sliced chillies (garnish)
fresh coriander (garnish)

1 Drain all the water from the bean curd and lift out the squares onto a double thickness of absorbent paper. Leave to drain thoroughly.

2 With a sharp knife remove the hard centre cabbage leaf ribs and cut in half if they are large. Plunge the leaves into boiling water to soften, then cool quickly in cold water. Drain well.

3 Plunge the spring onion tops into boiling water to soften, cool in cold water and set aside.

4 Heat the oil and fry the beef until it changes colour. Add a tablespoon each of the fish sauce and palm sugar. Add the Pepper and Coriander Paste and continue cooking until the meat is tender.

5 Mix in the bean curd and garlic chives. Reduce the heat and stir in the egg.

6 Cool slightly and divide the mixture between the cabbage leaves and roll up each one like a parcel, tucking in the ends. Secure each roll by tying with the softened spring onion tops.

7 Place the rolls in a pan and pour in the stock mixed with the Golden Mountain sauce and the remaining palm sugar. Simmer for 20–25 minutes, or until the cabbage is tender.

8 Drain the rolls and place on a serving plate. Blend the rice flour with the remaining tablespoon of fish sauce, mix into the stock and stir until thick. Stir in the lime juice, then pour over the rolls. Garnish with the sliced chillies and coriander.

# TEMPEH CURRY

## Lon Tempeh (Serves 4)

*Tempeh is a high-protein ingredient in vegetarian diets, made from fermented soybeans pressed into a cake. Look for it in the freezer section of Asian or health food stores, usually in 250 g (8 oz) packets.*

125 g (4 oz) **tempeh**
½ cup (4 fl oz) peanut oil
2 cups (16 fl oz) coconut milk
1 tablespoon Red Curry Paste
  (*page 3*)
½ teaspoon grated kaffir lime
  rind
6 spring onions, cut into short
  lengths
1 teaspoon palm sugar
1 tablespoon fish sauce
20 fresh basil leaves
¼ cup fresh coriander
  (garnish)
2 red or green chillies, sliced
  (garnish)

1 Thaw the *tempeh* if frozen, and slice thinly.

2 Heat the oil in a wok or frying pan and fry the *tempeh* until crisp and golden. Drain on absorbent paper.

3 Pour off the oil, wipe out the wok and heat half the coconut milk until boiling. Add the curry paste with the lime rind, and cook until fragrant.

4 Add the spring onions to the simmering mixture together with the fried *tempeh*. Stir in the remaining coconut milk and simmer, uncovered, for about 7 minutes. Stir in the palm sugar, fish sauce and basil leaves. Serve hot over noodles or with steamed jasmine rice, garnished with coriander leaves and chillies.

# FRIED BEAN CURD AND MIXED VEGETABLES

*Tao Hu Phad Pak Pason* (Serves 4)

*See colour plate on page 165.*

½ cup peeled pumpkin, cut
　　into 4 cm (1½ in) strips
½ cup celery, sliced
½ cup fresh asparagus, cut
　　into 4 cm (1½ in) lengths
1 × 425 g (13½ oz) can young
　　corn cobs, drained
½ cup snow peas (*mange-tout*),
　　strings removed
4 pieces black fungus, soaked
　　for 10 minutes
1 tablespoon peanut oil
1 teaspoon finely chopped
　　garlic
3–4 squares fried bean curd,
　　each cut into 8 pieces
1 tablespoon fish sauce or
　　light soy sauce
1 medium chilli, seeded and
　　finely sliced (garnish)

1 Prepare all the vegetables and have them ready in separate bowls. Trim any gritty pieces from the drained black fungus, then cut into pieces.

2 Heat the oil in a wok and fry the garlic until golden. Add the pumpkin and celery, and toss over heat for 4 or 5 minutes. Toss in the asparagus, corn cobs, snow peas, black fungus and bean curd, and stir-fry for a further 5 minutes.

3 Cover and cook on medium heat until the vegetables are tender but still crisp. Season with the fish sauce and garnish with sliced chillies. Serve with steamed jasmine rice or noodles.

# FRIED BEAN CURD IN COCONUT MILK

*Tao Hu Tom Kha* *(Serves 4–6)*

*This is a vegetarian version of the popular chicken dish,* Tom Kha Gai, *which features a galangal-flavoured coconut sauce.*

6 slices galangal
3 kaffir lime leaves
10 squares fried bean curd
2½ cups (20 fl oz) thin
   coconut milk
1 teaspoon Pepper and
   Coriander Paste (*page 8*)
2 stems lemon grass, thinly
   sliced
3 fresh green chillies
1 teaspoon salt
1 tablespoon fish sauce or
   light soy sauce
lime juice to taste
1 cup (8 fl oz) thick coconut
   milk
1 teaspoon sugar
¼ cup finely chopped fresh
   coriander (garnish)
2 red chillies, seeded and
   sliced (garnish)

1 If using dried galangal and kaffir lime leaves, soak them in hot water for 30 minutes.

2 Cut the squares of bean curd in half diagonally, then cut each piece in half again to give thin triangular slices.

3 Put the galangal, lime leaves, thin coconut milk, Pepper and Coriander Paste, lemon grass, green chillies, salt and fish sauce into a saucepan and bring gently to the boil, stirring. Simmer for 10 minutes, then add the bean curd and simmer for a further 10 minutes.

4 Stir in the lime juice, thick coconut milk and sugar, and continue simmering for a few minutes longer, until the sauce is thick and reduced. Sprinkle with the coriander and red chillies, and serve with steamed jasmine rice.

# EGGPLANT WITH BEAN CURD

*Phad Makua Tao Hu* (Serves 4–6)

250 g (8 oz) slender eggplants
   (aubergines)
3 tablespoons peanut oil
2 teaspoons finely chopped
   garlic
250 g (8 oz) soft bean curd,
   drained
1 teaspoon palm sugar
1 tablespoon lime juice
1 tablespoon fish sauce
4 red chillies, seeded and
   sliced
½ cup basil leaves

1 Wash the eggplants, but do not peel them. Cut the eggplants into thin slices on an angle.

2 Heat the oil in a wok, add the eggplants and garlic, and stir-fry until golden. Stir in the bean curd and cook a further 2 minutes, or until golden.

3 Gently stir in the combined palm sugar, lime juice, fish sauce, chillies and basil leaves. Serve as part of a meal with steamed jasmine rice and other dishes.

# EGGPLANT IN BATTER

*Makua Chup Pang Tod* (Serves 4)

2 slender eggplants
   (aubergines)
½ cup (2 oz) rice flour
½ teaspoon baking powder
½ teaspoon salt
1 egg yolk
½ cup (4 fl oz) coconut milk
peanut oil for deep-frying

1 Wash but do not peel the eggplants, then cut into thin diagonal slices.

2 In a bowl combine the rest of the ingredients except the oil, and whisk to a smooth batter. Dip the sliced eggplant in the batter and deep-fry until crisp. Drain and serve immediately with *nam prik* (*page 55*).

# STIR-FRIED EGGPLANT WITH *TEMPEH*

*Makua Phad Tempeh* (*Serves 4*)

125 g (4 oz) *tempeh*
3 tablespoons peanut oil
1 teaspoon finely chopped
   garlic
2 teaspoons Pepper and
   Coriander Paste (*page 8*)
250 g (8 oz) slender eggplants
   (aubergines), cut into 2 cm
   (¾ in) dice
1–2 tablespoons fish sauce or
   light soy sauce
1 teaspoon palm sugar
2 teaspoons lime juice
1 or 2 red chillies, finely
   sliced, or 2 whole red
   chillies, fried

1 Thaw the *tempeh* and steam for 10 minutes, then cut into thin slices.

2 Heat the oil and fry the garlic, and Pepper and Coriander Paste, stirring constantly, until fragrant.

3 Add the *tempeh* and fry until golden brown, then remove and set aside. Add the eggplants and fry until golden brown, adding more oil if necessary.

4 Stir in the fish sauce or soy sauce, palm sugar and lime juice, then return the fried *tempeh*. Mix together well and serve sprinkled with sliced chillies, or place a couple of fried whole chillies on top.

# FILLED AND FRIED EGGPLANT

*Makua Sod Sai Tod* (Serves 6)

*Slender eggplants (aubergines) that are no wider than a gherkin, though a little longer, are becoming more readily available here. They should be used for this recipe, not the large ones.*

6 slender young eggplants
  (aubergines)
125 g (4 oz) raw prawn
  (shrimp) meat
125 g (4 oz) chicken breast
  fillets
½ cup finely chopped spring
  onions
2 teaspoons finely chopped
  garlic
1 red or green chilli, finely
  chopped
1 tablespoon finely chopped
  coriander leaves
1 stem lemon grass, finely
  chopped
2 tablespoons fish sauce

BATTER
1 egg
3 tablespoons water
3 tablespoons rice flour
3 tablespoons plain (all-
  purpose) flour
peanut oil for deep-frying

1 Halve the eggplants lengthwise and sprinkle with salt. Leave for 20 minutes to degorge, then pat dry with absorbent paper. Scoop out the centres, leaving thin shells. Chop the centres finely and mix with the remaining ingredients. Fill the eggplants with the mixture, packing it in firmly.

2 TO MAKE THE BATTER, combine the egg, water and both kinds of flour.

3 Heat the oil in a wok or frying pan. Coat each eggplant with the batter and slide into the oil, then fry on medium-high heat until golden brown. Drain on absorbent paper and serve with Chilli Sauce (*page 54*).

# CABBAGE WITH PRAWNS AND PORK LOIN

*Moo Goong, Kalum Plee* (Serves 4–6)

250 g (8 oz) green cabbage
1 tablespoon peanut oil
1 teaspoon Pepper and
   Coriander Paste (*page 8*)
125 g (4 oz) pork loin or rib
   chop, diced
125 g (4 oz) raw prawns
   (shrimp), shelled and
   deveined
1 or 2 red chillies, seeded and
   sliced
1 teaspoon sugar
1 tablespoon fish sauce
1 teaspoon cornflour
   (cornstarch)

1  Trim the cabbage, removing the centre ribs if necessary and cut into approximately 2.5 × 5 cm (1 × 2 in) blocks.

2  Heat the oil and cook the paste for a minute or two. Add the pork and fry until crisp, then the prawns and stir-fry for 1 minute.

3  Stir in the cabbage and chillies, cover and cook for 3 or 4 minutes. Add the sugar and fish sauce. Thicken the liquid with cornflour blended with a tablespoon of cold water. Serve with steamed jasmine rice.

# CAULIFLOWER WITH THAI SPINACH

*Pad Pak Kom, Dok Galum* (Serves 4)

*Thai spinach (the same variety is used throughout Asia) is worth trying. If it is not available, use English spinach.*

125 g (4 oz) Thai spinach
2 coriander roots, chopped
1 teaspoon chopped garlic
½ teaspoon turmeric
1 tablespoon peanut oil
4 whole spring onions, cut
   into 4 cm (1½ in) lengths
125 g (4 oz) cauliflower,
   broken into florets
1 yellow or red chilli, sliced
   (garnish)

1 Wash the spinach, cut into 8 cm (3 in) lengths and blanch for a few seconds in boiling water, then refresh in cold water.

2 Pound the coriander roots to a paste in a mortar and pestle together with the garlic and turmeric. Heat half the oil and fry the spring onions for a minute. Add the spinach and toss for a further minute. Remove and set aside.

3 Heat the remaining oil and cook the coriander paste, stirring, until fragrant. Add the cauliflower and stir-fry for 4 or 5 minutes. Arrange on a dish, place the spinach and spring onions around, and serve garnished with sliced chilli.

# STIR-FRIED ASPARAGUS

*Phad Nor Mai Farang (Serves 4)*

*I always thought of asparagus as a very European vegetable, and was surprised to see some of the freshest, greenest, highest quality asparagus in the markets in Thailand.*

500 g (1 lb) asparagus
2 cloves finely chopped garlic
1 teaspoon green peppercorns, crushed
1 tablespoon fish sauce
1–2 tablespoons Golden Mountain sauce (*page 209*) or oyster sauce
2 teaspoons sugar
2 tablespoons peanut oil
2 red chillies, seeded and finely sliced

1 Trim the asparagus and peel the lower stalks. Cut into bite-sized pieces.

2 Combine the garlic, peppercorns, sauces and sugar, stirring to dissolve the sugar.

3 Heat the oil in a wok or frying pan, and on high heat stir-fry the asparagus until crisp and tender. Add the garlic mixture and chillies, mix well and serve at once.

# STIR-FRIED SPINACH

*Phad Pak Kom* (Serves 4)

500 g (1 lb) spinach
2 tablespoons peanut oil
1 teaspoon finely chopped
    garlic
½ cup sliced spring onions
¼ teaspoon freshly ground
    black pepper
2 tablespoons Golden
    Mountain sauce (*page 209*)
1 red chilli, seeded and finely
    sliced (garnish)

1  Wash the spinach well and remove the tough stems.

2  Heat the oil and cook the garlic and spring onions until golden. Add the spinach and gently stir-fry until just wilted.

3  Sprinkle over the pepper and Golden Mountain sauce. Garnish with the sliced chillies and serve immediately as spinach is very sensitive to heat, and will darken unattractively if left to stand.

# STIR-FRIED WATER CHESTNUTS AND SNOW PEAS

*Pad Haeo Chine, Tua Lun Tao* (Serves 4–6)

125 g (4 oz) snow peas
(*mange-tout*)
1 × 185 g (6 oz) can sliced
water chestnuts
2 tablespoons peanut oil
1 teaspoon finely chopped
garlic
1 tablespoon fish sauce
1 tablespoon Golden
Mountain sauce (*page 209*)
1 teaspoon sugar
½ cup (4 fl oz) stock or water
2 teaspoons cornflour
(cornstarch)

1 String the snow peas and drain the liquid from the water chestnuts. If unable to purchase them already sliced, cut the water chestnuts into two or three discs.

2 Heat the oil in a wok or frying pan and on a low heat fry the garlic, stirring, until it is just starting to change colour. Add the snow peas and toss for 1 minute, then add the water chestnuts, and the sauces, sugar and stock stirred together.

3 When it comes to the boil, stir in the cornflour mixed with a tablespoon of cold water. Stir constantly until it boils and thickens. Serve with steamed jasmine rice.

# WATER CONVOLVULUS WITH DRIED SHRIMP

*Pak Boong Phad Goong Haeng* (Serves 4)

*See colour plate on page 165.*

250 g (8 oz) water convolvulus
  (*kangkung*)
½ cup dried shrimp
1 tablespoon peanut oil
1 teaspoon finely chopped
  garlic
1 teaspoon finely chopped
  fresh ginger
1 tablespoon oyster sauce

1 Wash the vegetable well, shake off any surplus water and cut into 5 cm (2 in) lengths.

2 Soak the dried shrimp in hot water for about 10 minutes, drain, and pound lightly in a mortar and pestle.

3 Heat the oil and cook the garlic and ginger until golden. Stir in the shrimp and water convolvulus, and stir-fry for a couple of minutes until the leaves are wilted. Stir in the oyster sauce and serve immediately with steamed jasmine rice.

# RIDGED GOURD CURRY

## Gaeng Khiew Wan Buab Liam *(Serves 4–5)*

*If you see this vegetable at the markets or in Asian stores, be prepared to give it a try – it is mild and sweet, and blends well with coconut milk and fresh herbs.*

1 ridged gourd, about 150 g (5 oz)

1 cup (8 fl oz) thick coconut milk

2 teaspoons Green Curry Paste (*page 4*)

1 tablespoon finely sliced lemon grass

1 tablespoon fish sauce

½ cup (4 fl oz) water

2 teaspoons lime juice

1 teaspoon palm sugar

1 or 2 fresh green chillies

1 Wash the gourd well and use a vegetable peeler to remove the sharp edges from the ridges that run down the length of the vegetable. Cut into 4 cm (1½ in) slices.

2 Heat ½ cup (4 fl oz) of the coconut milk, add the paste and cook, stirring, until fragrant. Add the lemon grass, fish sauce and water. Stir until it comes to the boil, then simmer for 2 to 3 minutes.

3 Add the slices of gourd, lime juice, palm sugar and green chillies, and simmer until the gourd is tender. Stir in the remaining ½ cup coconut milk, heat through and serve with steamed jasmine rice or noodles.

# STUFFED ZUCCHINI

*Sod Sai Zucchini* (Serves 4–6)

*Choose zucchini (courgettes) that are about 6–7 cm (2½–3 in) in diameter so there is room for an adequate amount of filling.*

2 or 3 medium-large zucchini
    (courgettes)
kaffir lime leaf, shredded
    (garnish)
chilli slices (garnish)

**FILLING**
250 g (8 oz) minced (ground)
    pork
125 g (4 oz) raw prawns
    (shrimp), shelled, deveined
    and chopped
¼ teaspoon finely grated lime
    rind
1 tablespoon fish sauce
1 teaspoon palm sugar
½ cup finely chopped spring
    onions
2 teaspoons Pepper and
    Coriander Paste (*page 8*)

**COCONUT SAUCE**
¾ cup (6 fl oz) coconut milk
½ teaspoon salt
2 teaspoons rice flour

1 Wash the zucchini, top and tail them, then cut into 4 cm (1½ in) slices. Scoop out the centre of each slice, leaving a thin layer on the bottom as a base.

2 **TO MAKE THE FILLING**, combine all the ingredients and fill each zucchini slice with 2 to 3 teaspoons of mixture. Steam for 15–20 minutes, or until cooked through but still holding their shape. Arrange on a serving plate.

3 **TO MAKE THE COCONUT SAUCE**, combine all the ingredients in a small saucepan and cook, stirring, until it comes to the boil and thickens. Spoon the sauce over the slices and garnish with fine shreds of lime leaf and chilli slices.

*Water convolvulus with dried shrimp (page 162),*
*Fried bean curd and mixed vegetables (page 152).*

Floating market soup noodles (page 175)

# RICE AND NOODLES

*P*lain jasmine rice, perfectly steamed, is the single most important item in Thai meals. Whatever else is served is termed 'with the rice'. Fried rice with all its additions is a snack eaten on its own and not the central dish in a meal.

There is no trick to cooking perfect, fluffy rice. It is all a matter of correct proportions, and if the same cup is used to measure rice and water, all will be well. For best results, use first grade, long grain 'jasmine' rice grown in Thailand. It has a faint natural perfume and the grains remain separate. No salt is added as the accompanying sauces are usually salty enough.

If you cook rice often, do yourself a favour and get a rice cooker, which is readily available from most large stores or Asian food stores.

Noodles in Thailand come in a host of different sizes, and are made from rice flour, mung bean starch, wheat flour and eggs. Rice noodles are the most popular in Thailand, and are freshly made each day, but dried rice noodles are perfectly acceptable for home use and have a longer shelf life.

# STEAMED JASMINE RICE (ABSORPTION METHOD)

*Khao* (Serves 4–6)

*Cooking rice by absorption in a pan with a well-fitting lid is both quick and easy, but it is essential that the heat can be turned very low, because the rice can stick to the pan and scorch.*

**2½ cups (1 lb) long grain rice**
**3½ cups (28 fl oz) water**

**NOTE** *If the rice is to be used for fried rice, turn it out onto a large tray as soon as cooking is completed, and leave to become completely cold and dry. Refrigerate overnight, uncovered, for the best results.*

1 Put the rice and water into a heavy-based pan, bring to the boil, then cover tightly and turn the heat as low as it will go. Cook without lifting the lid for 15 minutes. The water should be completely absorbed.

2 Remove from heat, uncover and let the steam escape for a few minutes, then replace the lid to keep the rice warm.

# MIXED FRIED RICE

*Khao Phat Ruam Mit (Serves 4)*

*Making fried rice is like jazz improvisation – anything goes. Well, almost anything. This recipe is offered as a guide, but feel free to substitute ingredients as available.*

3 eggs, beaten
salt and pepper
3 tablespoons peanut oil
1 onion, finely chopped
1 teaspoon crushed garlic
2 fresh hot chillies, seeded
   and sliced
1 pork chop, finely diced or
   1 chicken breast, diced
250 g (8 oz) raw prawns
   (shrimp)
4 cups cold cooked rice
125 g (4 oz) frozen crab meat,
   or meat from 1 cooked crab
2 tablespoons fish sauce or to
   taste
2 tablespoons chilli sauce or
   to taste
chilli flower (garnish)

1 Season the eggs with salt and pepper to taste. Heat a wok or frying pan and grease lightly with 1 teaspoon of the oil. Pour in some of the beaten egg, swirl to coat the pan and cook over low heat until set but not browned. Remove to a plate and repeat with the remaining beaten egg. Set aside to cool, then roll up and cut into fine strips.

2 Heat the remaining oil in the wok and fry the onion and garlic, stirring frequently, until golden. Add half the sliced chillies and toss for a few seconds, then fry the diced pork or chicken until well cooked.

3 Add the prawns and stir-fry until they change colour. Add the rice and toss over high heat until heated through. Add the crab meat, fish sauce and chilli sauce and toss constantly for a further minute or two. Serve sprinkled with the remaining sliced chillies and garnished with the omelette strips and a chilli flower.

# CRAB FRIED RICE IN OMELETTE

*Kai Yud Sai Khao Poo* (Serves 4)

2 tablespoons peanut oil
4 spring onions, chopped
2 fresh chillies, seeded and
sliced
1 tablespoon Red Curry Paste
(*page 3*)
125 g (4 oz) uncooked
medium-sized prawns
(shrimp), shelled and
deveined
1 cup fresh or frozen crab
meat
2 cups cold steamed rice
1 tablespoon fish sauce
1 tablespoon lime or lemon
juice
1 clove garlic, crushed
spring onion tops

OMELETTES
8 eggs
½ teaspoon salt
2 tablespoons water
2 tablespoons peanut oil

1  Heat a wok, pour in the oil and on medium heat fry the spring onions and chillies, stirring, until softened. Add the curry paste and cook, stirring, until fragrant.

2  Add the prawns and stir-fry until they change colour. Stir in the crab meat and rice, tossing until heated through. Remove from the heat.

3  Combine the fish sauce, lime or lemon juice and garlic, and sprinkle over the rice, tossing to distribute the seasoning. Put the rice in a bowl, cover and keep warm. Wash and dry the wok.

4  **TO MAKE THE OMELETTES,** beat the eggs with the salt and water. Heat the wok or a large frying pan, add 2 teaspoons of the oil and swirl to coat the surface. Pour in a quarter of the beaten egg mixture and swirl to make a large sheet of egg of even thickness. Cook over low heat until almost set.

5  Place a quarter of the rice mixture in the centre of the omelette and fold the edges over, envelope fashion, to enclose the rice. Press down well, slip a frying slice (wide metal spatula) underneath and gently turn over. Drizzle a little oil down the side of the wok and lightly brown the other side. Lift onto a plate. Repeat with the remaining mixture.

6  Dip the spring onion tops in boiling water until limp, and use to tie each omelette parcel.

# ICED RICE

*Khao Chae (Serves 4)*

*This is an example of palace cooking that has become accessible to everyone. When it was devised by the ladies of King Chulalongkorn's court, ice was a luxury because it had to be brought in by ship from Singapore. In hot weather, rice was served in water scented with jasmine and rose petals and crushed ice. Today, one can buy this dish at more plebian food stalls. But, as of old, the highly flavoured dishes accompanying the rice are intended to tempt jaded appetites.*

3 cups (24 fl oz) ice water
12–15 jasmine flowers
petals from 1 fragrant rose
4 cups cold cooked rice
crushed ice

ACCOMPANIMENTS
Fried Prawn Balls (*page 128*)
Sweet and Hot Crisp Beef
   (*page 126*)
Pork-stuffed Capsicum in Egg
   Net (*page 19*)

1 Have the accompaniments prepared and ready. If possible, let the flowers steep in the water overnight, in a covered bowl in the refrigerator. Alternatively, add a few drops of jasmine or rose essence to the water.

2 Put the completely cold rice in a serving bowl, pour the scented water over and add the crushed ice and a few blossoms. Serve, before the ice melts, with the accompaniments.

# DEEP-FRIED RICE CRACKERS

*Khao Tang-Na Tang* (Serves 8)

*If the rice sticks at the bottom of the pot, Thai cooks turn it into a delicious snack. It is so popular that it is now a dish in its own right.*

**1 cup (6 oz) short grain rice**
**1½ cups (12 fl oz) water**
**peanut oil for deep-frying**

1 Put the rice and water in a saucepan and boil, uncovered, until holes appear in the rice mass. Turn the heat to very low, cover the pan tightly and cook for 15 minutes. Cool.

2 Grease a large tray, spread the rice out on the tray and flatten to a thin layer with a hand dipped in water. Mark into triangles or squares with a wet knife and bake in a very slow oven, 130°C (275°F/Gas 2), until completely dry, about 1 hour.

3 Remove from the oven and cool. Break into the marked pieces, and store in an airtight container. Just before serving, deep-fry in hot oil until golden and puffed. Drain on absorbent paper. Serve with Shrimp Dip with Tamarind (*page 58*) and/or Pork and Peanut Dip (*page 56*).

# RICE AND COCONUT PANCAKES

*Khanom Krok (Makes about 24)*

*These creamy rice cakes are baked in a pan that has round indentations similar to a gem iron, used for gem scones in Australia; or an* aebelskiver *pan, which Danish cooks use and which is probably more common in Europe and the United States. They may be placed over a gas flame or electric hotplate.*

1 cup (6 oz) uncooked rice
4 tablespoons cooked rice
1 cup grated fresh coconut
pinch of salt
1 tablespoon sugar
3 cups (24 fl oz) boiling water
½ cup (4 fl oz) thick coconut
   milk
2 tablespoons sugar
¼ teaspoon salt
peanut oil

TOPPING
2 tablespoons chopped spring
   onions
2 tablespoons corn kernels
2 tablespoons pounded dried
   shrimp (optional)

1  Put the first 5 ingredients into a bowl and pour the boiling water over. When cold, blend at high speed in an electric blender until very finely ground.

2  Mix the coconut milk, sugar and salt together.

3  Heat the gem iron or similar pan and brush with oil. Pour a small ladle of the rice mixture into each hollow to almost fill the pan. Cook over low heat or in a hot oven at 220°C (425°F/Gas 7), until the surface is firm. Top each with a teaspoon of the coconut milk mixture. Add a sprinkling of chopped spring onions, a few corn kernels or some dried shrimp powder and finish by cooking a further minute or two in the oven. Run a small spatula between the pan and each cake to loosen, and if the outside is well browned and crisp, remove to a wire rack. Serve warm.

# PORK BALLS WITH NOODLES

*Ba Mee Look Chin Moo* (Serves 4)

2 dried shiitake mushrooms
250 g (8 oz) minced (ground) pork
1 teaspoon Pepper and Coriander Paste (*page 8*)
2 tablespoons finely chopped bamboo shoots
2 tablespoons finely chopped water chestnuts
1 tablespoon plain (all-purpose) flour
2 bundles egg noodles, about 100 g (3½ oz)

CURRY

1½ cups (12 fl oz) coconut milk
1 tablespoon Green Curry Paste (*page 4*)
2 teaspoons finely chopped garlic
2 teaspoons fish sauce
1 tablespoon seeded and sliced chillies
1 teaspoon palm sugar
3 tablespoons sliced spring onions (garnish)
fresh coriander (garnish)
chilli flowers (garnish)

1  Soak the mushrooms in hot water for at least 30 minutes. Drain and chop finely. Put into a bowl with the next 5 ingredients and mix well. Shape the mixture into small balls about 4 cm (1½ in) in diameter and set aside.

2  Cook the noodles in fast boiling water until tender, drain and rinse in cold water.

3  TO MAKE THE CURRY, heat half of the coconut milk in a wok. Stir in the curry paste and garlic, and cook until fragrant. Stir in the remaining coconut milk and when boiling, drop in a few pork balls at a time. Reduce the heat and simmer the pork balls for 8 to 10 minutes.

4  Gently stir in the fish sauce, chillies and palm sugar. Drain the noodles and gently stir into the curry. Cook for 2–3 minutes. Serve hot, garnished with spring onions, coriander leaves and chilli flowers. It may be necessary to add more coconut milk or hot water if the curry is too thick.

# FLOATING MARKET SOUP NOODLES

*Kway Teo Ruer* (Serves 4)

*These noodles will always remind me of breakfast at the floating market at Damnernsaduak. Sitting on wooden steps leading down to the canal and eating the noodles with chopsticks, we enjoyed watching the lady vendor deftly cook each serving separately. Wearing the typical wide-brimmed bamboo hat, she gracefully balanced herself in her boat as it swayed and dipped in the wash of other boats going past and was delighted when we asked for the accompaniments of hot chillies and salty* nam pla *just like the local customers. Fried shallots (sometimes labelled 'red onions') may be bought in ready-to-use tubs or packets. Store in the freezer. They will not need heating. See colour plate on page 166.*

6 cups (1.5 litres/48 fl oz) pork
   or chicken Stock (*page 34*)
125 g (4 oz) minced (ground)
   pork
125 g (4 oz) chicken or pork,
   finely sliced
2 tablespoons dried shrimp
2 or 3 cubes fried bean curd,
   sliced
125 g (4 oz) rice noodles,
   soaked and drained
2 teaspoons palm sugar
2 tablespoons fish sauce
2 tablespoons lime juice
1 cup bean sprouts

ACCOMPANIMENTS
2 tablespoons preserved
   radish, shredded
¼ cup roasted peanuts,
   crushed
½ cup chopped fresh
   coriander
1 tablespoon crisp-fried garlic
   flakes
2 tablespoons fried shallots
sliced hot chillies in fish sauce
dried chillies, crushed
   (optional)

1 Bring 1 cup (8 fl oz) of the stock to the boil, add the minced pork and stir while cooking to break up any lumps. Add the sliced chicken or pork and the remaining stock, and simmer until tender.

2 Add the dried shrimp, bean curd and rice noodles. Stir in the palm sugar, fish sauce, lime juice and bean sprouts. Simmer for 2 minutes. Taste and add more fish sauce or lime juice if necessary.

3 Serve the noodles and soup in bowls, topped with a little of each of the accompaniments, and let each person help themselves to the chillies.

# FRIED EGG NOODLES WITH BARBECUED PORK

*Ba Mee Phat Moo Yang (Serves 4–6)*

*The Chinese influence shows through in this dish, tempered by the ever-present Thai flavourings of chilli, fish sauce and lime juice.*

4 dried shiitake mushrooms
1 cup (8 fl oz) hot water
2 tablespoons soy sauce
2 teaspoons sugar
1 tablespoon salted black
  beans
5 bundles thin egg noodles
3 tablespoons peanut oil
1 teaspoon finely chopped
  garlic
1 teaspoon finely grated fresh
  ginger
3 fresh chillies, sliced
150 g (5 oz) barbecued pork,
  thinly sliced
3 whole spring onions, sliced
2 tablespoons fish sauce
2 tablespoons lime juice

ACCOMPANIMENTS
crisp-fried onions
roasted peanuts, crushed
dried chillies, crushed
fresh chillies, sliced
2 tablespoons fish sauce
2 tablespoons lime juice
1 teaspoon sugar

**NOTE** *Crisp-fried onions may be bought from Asian food stores. Store in the freezer. Thin egg noodles are sold in packets. Barbecued pork can be purchased in Chinese restaurants.*

1 Soak the dried mushrooms in the water for 30 minutes, then drain, reserving the water. Discard the stems. Slice the caps and simmer for 15 minutes in the soaking water with the soy sauce and sugar.

2 Rinse the salted black beans in a small strainer under the cold tap for a few seconds to remove excess salt.

3 Put water on to boil for cooking the noodles. Place the noodles in a bowl, run hot water from the tap to cover them and leave to soak for 10 minutes or until the strands separate. Drain, and drop into the boiling water. Cook for 2 or 3 minutes, until just tender. Drain well.

4 Heat the oil in a wok and fry the garlic and ginger for a few seconds without browning. Add the black beans and chillies and fry for a few minutes. Toss in the noodles, barbecued pork, mushrooms and spring onions, sprinkle with the fish sauce and lime juice and toss until evenly mixed. Serve with the accompaniments in small bowls – the first three are kept separate, and the sliced fresh chillies are mixed with the fish sauce, lime juice and sugar.

# RICE NOODLES WITH CHICKEN AND PRAWNS

*Kway Teo Phat Gai Goong* (Serves 4)

125 g (4 oz) rice sticks
250 g (8 oz) chicken thigh
   fillets
3 tablespoons peanut oil
1 teaspoon crushed garlic
½ cup tiny dried shrimp
2 teaspoons chilli radish,
   chopped
1 teaspoon black bean sauce
   with chilli (*page 180*)
2 tablespoons fish sauce
1 tablespoon chilli sauce
1 tablespoon lime juice
½ cup chopped fresh
   coriander
½ cup roasted, salted peanuts,
   chopped

1  Pour boiling water over the rice sticks, cover and allow to soak for 10 minutes. Drain in a colander.

2  Remove the skin and any visible fat from the chicken, and cut the flesh into thin slices.

3  Heat a wok or frying pan, add the oil and fry the garlic until golden, stirring constantly. Add the dried shrimp and fry, stirring, for 1 minute.

4  Add the chilli radish and black bean sauce, stir well and turn in the chicken. Stir-fry until the chicken has changed colour.

5  Mix together the fish sauce, chilli sauce and lime juice and pour over the chicken. Toss in the rice noodles, mixing well. Mix half of the coriander and peanuts through and toss. Serve hot and use the remaining coriander and peanuts as garnishes.

# BEAN STARCH NOODLES WITH CHICKEN

*Kai Phad Woon Sen (Serves 2–3)*

*Thai food is so full of flavour, it is possible to make a light meal for two or three people using the quantity of meat or poultry that would feed one person in a Western-style dish.*

1 × 100 g (3½ oz) packet bean
   starch vermicelli
185 g (6 oz) chicken thigh
   fillets
½ teaspoon crushed garlic
2 teaspoons hot pickled
   bamboo shoots
1 onion, finely sliced
2 tablespoons dried shrimp
   (either tiny ones in shells or
   larger dried shrimp,
   pounded)
¼ cup roughly chopped spring
   onions or garlic chives
3 tablespoons peanut oil
1 egg, lightly beaten

SEASONING
1 tablespoon sweet chilli sauce
2 tablespoons fish sauce
1 teaspoon sugar
2 tablespoons lime juice

GARNISH
¼ cup fresh coriander
½ cup crushed roasted
   peanuts
1 red chilli, seeded and finely
   sliced or 1 teaspoon
   crushed dried chilli

1 Drop the noodles into boiling water and cook for 10 minutes to soften. Drain in a colander and cut into short lengths.

2 Remove all skin and fat from the chicken and cut the meat into fine slices.

3 Put the garlic, bamboo shoots and onion on a plate in separate mounds. Have the dried shrimp and spring onions or chives measured in small bowls.

4 Combine the seasoning ingredients in a bowl and stir to dissolve the sugar.

5 Heat a wok and add the oil. Add the garlic and stir-fry for a few seconds, then add the bamboo shoot and onion and continue to fry for a minute longer. Add the dried shrimp and spring onions, fry for 30 seconds and then add the chicken, turning it constantly until all the pinkness has disappeared and it is cooked. With this small amount of chicken, it should take only 2 minutes on high heat.

6 Add the seasoning and egg and stir well, turn in the noodles and keep tossing until evenly mixed. Add half the garnish ingredients and stir through. Serve sprinkled with the remaining garnishes.

# DEEP-FRIED CRISPY RICE NOODLES

*Mee Grob* (Serves 4)

*This is* Mee Grob, *the dish by which a good Thai restaurant is often judged. The noodles should be snapping crisp, the flavours prominently sweet, hot, salty and sour, with more than a suspicion of garlic making impact. Many restaurants concentrate on the sweet flavour, which is a pity.*

125 g (4 oz) rice vermicelli
3 cups (24 fl oz) peanut oil for deep-frying
½ cup finely minced (ground) pork or chicken
½ cup chopped prawns (shrimp)
1 cake yellow bean curd, finely diced
2 tablespoons white vinegar
2 tablespoons sugar
2 tablespoons fish sauce
2 eggs, beaten
2 tablespoons sliced pickled garlic
1 red chilli, finely sliced
½ cup fresh coriander

1 Dip the rice vermicelli quickly in cold water, shake off the excess and leave it near a window to dry for at least 30 minutes. Separate into small handfuls.

2 Heat the oil in a wok and when smoking test the heat with a few strands of the noodles. They should puff and swell to many times their size. If they don't, wait until the oil is hot enough or the noodles will be tough instead of crisp and light. Be ready to scoop them out as soon as they turn pale golden and drain well on several sheets of absorbent paper. Cool completely.

3 Pour off the excess oil, leaving only about 2 tablespoons in the wok. Add the pork or chicken and fry, stirring constantly, until they change colour.

4 Add the prawns and cook for a further minute, then add the bean curd and toss until heated through. Add the vinegar, sugar and fish sauce, stirred together until the sugar has dissolved. When the mixture boils add the beaten eggs and keep on stirring until the egg is set and firm. This recipe may be prepared ahead to this stage, but heat through before serving.

5 Just before serving, combine the crisp-fried noodles with the hot mixture. Scatter the pickled garlic, chilli and coriander leaves over and serve immediately.

# RICE NOODLES WITH HOT SEASONINGS

*Sen Mee Phat Nuer* (Serves 4)

250 g (8 oz) rice vermicelli
3 tablespoons peanut oil
1 teaspoon chopped garlic
2 teaspoons fermented soy-
  bean with sesame
½ teaspoon black bean sauce
  with chilli (*see* Note)
185 g (6 oz) chicken or beef,
  finely shredded

SEASONING
1 tablespoon sweet chilli sauce
2 tablespoons fish sauce
1 tablespoon lime juice

GARNISH
¼ cup chopped fresh
  coriander
1 tablespoon crisp-fried garlic
  flakes (*page 208*)
1 teaspoon dried chilli flakes

NOTE *'Black bean sauce with chilli' is
my description of an ingredient which
is known – apart from the Oriental
characters – by the French name* sauce
de soja au piment. *It is very hot, and
should be approached with caution!
The fermented soybeans with sesame
are also sold in jars in Asian stores.*

1  Put the rice vermicelli in a bowl and run very hot water from the tap to cover. Soak for 10 minutes, then drain. Measure the other ingredients and have everything ready to hand. Mix all the seasoning ingredients together.

2  Heat a wok, add the oil, and fry the garlic until golden, stirring constantly. Add the fermented beans and the black bean sauce and stir quickly. Then add the chicken or beef and cook until it changes colour.

3  Pour in the seasoning mixture, stir and allow to come to the boil. Turn in the drained vermicelli and mix thoroughly with half of the garnish ingredients. Sprinkle the remaining garnishes on top before serving.

# WHOLE EARTH VEGETARIAN NOODLES

*Phat Mee Jeh* (Serves 4)

*This recipe is reconstructed from memory after a delicious vegetarian meal at the Whole Earth restaurant in Chiang Mai, and has been taste-tested at home.*

250 g (8 oz) fine rice
    vermicelli
6 dried shiitake mushrooms
2 tablespoons wood fungus
125 g (4 oz) fried bean curd
    squares or fermented
    soybean (*tempeh*)
125 g (4 oz) fresh bean sprouts
1 cup fine julienne of carrot
a few tender asparagus tips,
    blanched
2 cups finely shredded
    cabbage
3 tablespoons peanut oil
1 teaspoon crushed garlic
1 teaspoon finely grated fresh
    ginger
2 tablespoons Golden
    Mountain sauce (*page 209*)
    or light soy sauce
2 teaspoons sugar
extra chilli sauce
radish flower (garnish)

1 Put the noodles into a bowl and pour boiling water over. Leave to soak for 2 or 3 minutes, then drain. Test by biting a piece – it should be soft but still have some bite. The very fine variety will be done in a shorter time.

2 Soak the dried mushrooms in very hot water for 30 minutes, squeeze out any excess water, discard the stems and cut the caps into thin strips. Soak the wood fungus in cold water for 10 minutes, cut off any gritty portions, and divide into bite-sized pieces.

3 Dice or slice the bean curd or, if using *tempeh*, cut in thin slices and then into fine strips. Wash and drain the bean sprouts and pinch off any straggly tails. Set all these ingredients and the vegetables on a plate in separate piles, reserving some bean sprouts and shredded cabbage for garnish.

4 Heat a wok, add the oil and swirl to coat the wok. On medium heat fry the garlic and ginger, stirring, until golden (about 1 minute). Add the bean curd or *tempeh* and fry. Add the mushrooms and ½ cup (4 fl oz) water, then stir in the Golden Mountain or light soy sauce and sugar and simmer for 10 minutes. There should be about ¼ cup (2 fl oz) liquid. If necessary add a little more water.

5 Add the wood fungus and all the vegetables and toss for a minute, then turn in the noodles and mix well. Cover and steam for 3 or 4 minutes to heat through. Toss vigorously again to mix all the ingredients and serve hot, garnished with the reserved bean sprouts, shredded cabbage, and a radish flower. Chilli sauce is served separately as a flavour accent.

# GLASS NOODLES WITH PRAWNS

*Goong Phad Woon Sen* (Serves 6–8)

*Because they are so transparent, bean starch noodles have attracted different names such as 'glass noodles'. Usually called 'mung bean thread' on the packet or 'spring rain noodles', the more prosaic term is 'bean thread vermicelli'. This recipe may be prepared with either, but I prefer the flatter and somewhat broader noodle as it holds the sauce better.*

1 × 225 g (8 oz) packet mung
   bean thread
3 tablespoons peanut oil
½ cup Red Curry Paste
   (*page 3*)
500 g (1 lb) raw prawns,
   shelled and deveined
1–2 tablespoons fish sauce
½ cup roasted salted peanuts,
   roughly chopped
¼ cup chopped spring onions
¼ cup chopped fresh
   coriander

1 Drop the noodles into a large saucepan of boiling water for about 8 minutes or until cooked but still retaining its bite. Tip into a colander and run cold water through to stop cooking. Run a knife through to make shorter lengths for easier handling.

2 Heat a wok, add the oil and fry the curry paste on low heat, stirring, until fragrant. Add the prawns, cut into smaller pieces if large, and stir-fry in the paste until the prawns turn opaque and are cooked.

3 Add the noodles and toss until they are evenly coated with the curry paste. Sprinkle over the fish sauce and toss again to distribute the flavours.

4 Turn off the heat, pile the noodles and prawns in a bowl and sprinkle with the peanuts, spring onions and fresh coriander. Serve at once.

*Agar-agar jellies (page 186).*

*Tempting Thai desserts*
*clockwise from top:*
*Mangoes with sweet rice (page 191),*
*Bananas in sago cream (page 187),*
*Agar-agar jellies (page 186).*

# DESSERTS AND SWEET SNACKS

As in most Asian cuisines, desserts are not a feature of Thai meals but there is no denying that most people like to finish a meal with something sweet, be it fresh fruit or fruit juice or one of the fancier recipes featured here.

For the most part, these sweets are eaten as between-meal snacks. They are based mainly on rice flour or tapioca flour, coconut milk, palm sugar, mung beans and vegetables such as pumpkin and potato. Strongly flavoured fruits like mango and durian also feature. Unless indicated, use a bland vegetable oil when making desserts.

Most of these desserts are dainty mouthfuls and quite irresistible. Some of them are so simple that they can be made in almost no time compared to Western desserts. Others are fun to make if you have a little time to spare – for example, moulding the miniature fruits. Making them is as enjoyable as eating them!

# AGAR-AGAR JELLIES

*Woon* (Makes about 30 tiny jellies)

*Agar-agar is refined from seaweed and gives a clear, firm jelly which will not melt even in tropical heat. If you're ever in Thailand, go into a department store and buy some miniature jelly moulds. Otherwise, use small French tartlet moulds or foil cups for the jellies. See colour plate on page 183.*

2 cups (16 fl oz) water
2 teaspoons agar-agar powder
⅓ cup (3 oz) white sugar
red, green and blue food
    colouring
rose or jasmine essence
*pandan* (*bai toey*) essence
1 tablespoon coconut milk or
    evaporated milk
salt

1 Pour the water into a saucepan and sprinkle the agar-agar powder over the surface. Bring slowly to the boil and stir until the agar-agar is completely dissolved.

2 Add the sugar and stir until it dissolves. Remove from the heat and divide the mixture into 4 bowls.

3 Colour and flavour the other three as desired, leaving one portion plain. Into the plain portion stir the coconut milk and a tiny pinch of salt to accentuate the flavour of the coconut.

4 Pour into small moulds. If making more than one layer, place the moulds in the refrigerator to set while you keep the rest of the jelly warm in a pan of simmering water. When the first layer has set, add the next. When set, slip them out of the moulds with gentle pressure on one side. Turn the shapes upside down on the serving plate. It is quite in order to pick them up with the fingers for eating.

5 If small moulds are not available, use tiny confectionery cups to set the jellies. If the cups are of waxed paper, use two or three together for stability. Foil cups hold their shape better.

# BANANAS IN SAGO CREAM

*Gluay Saku Kati* (Serves 4)

*Use whichever variety of sago or tapioca you prefer. If using the instant quick-cooking variety, follow the instructions on the packet. See colour plate on page 184.*

1.5 litres (6 cups) water
½ cup (3 oz) sago or tapioca
1 cup (8 fl oz) water
⅓ cup (3 oz) white sugar
1 tablespoon palm sugar
2 cups (16 fl oz) coconut milk
¼ teaspoon salt
3 or 4 bananas

1 In a large saucepan bring the water to a boil and sprinkle in the sago or tapioca. Boil for 7 minutes for small grains, or 15 minutes for the large. Turn off the heat, cover with a tight-fitting lid and allow to stand for a further 10–15 minutes. By this time, the grains should be perfectly clear. Run cold water into the pan and strain through a fine sieve. Hold the sieve under the cold tap to rinse away the excess starch.

2 Combine the 1 cup (8 fl oz) water with the sugar and palm sugar and stir until boiling. Simmer for 5 minutes, then stir in the coconut milk and salt. Remove from the heat and stir in the sago or tapioca.

3 Peel the bananas and slice thickly, holding the knife at a slight angle. Put a few slices of banana in each bowl and ladle the coconut milk and sago mixture over. Serve warm or at room temperature.

# BANANAS IN SWEET COCONUT MILK

*Gluay Buad Chee* (Serves 4)

*This simple dessert is one of the more popular desserts served in restaurants.*

3 or 4 ladies' finger bananas
2 cups (16 fl oz) coconut milk
4 tablespoons white sugar
pinch of salt

1 Peel the bananas and cut into bite-sized pieces. Dilute the coconut milk with 1 cup (8 fl oz) water if using the canned variety and put into a saucepan with the sugar and salt. Stir until boiling, then boil for 2 minutes.

2 Add the banana pieces and simmer over low heat for 2 minutes, or until the bananas are soft but still retain their shape. They may be cooked longer if a softer result is preferred, but they do lose their texture. Serve warm.

# BANANAS IN COCONUT CREAM

*Gluay Khao Poad Gaeng Buad* (Serves 4–6)

*Many Asian desserts are fairly liquid mixtures and this is one of the most popular.*

½ cup (4 oz) white sugar
2 tablespoons palm sugar
  (optional)
1 cup (8 fl oz) water
3 cups (24 fl oz) fresh coconut
  milk or 2 cups (16 fl oz)
  canned coconut milk and
  1 cup (8 fl oz) water
1 cup tender corn kernels
  sliced from the cob or
  drained canned corn
3 or 4 ripe bananas, cut into
  chunks
2 drops jasmine essence
1 tablespoon toasted sesame
  seeds (optional)

1 Make a syrup with the sugar, palm sugar and water. Add the coconut milk, corn and bananas and simmer uncovered for 5 minutes. Remove from the heat and cool to lukewarm.

2 Stir in the jasmine essence and spoon into bowls. Serve slightly warm or at room temperature, with a sprinkling of toasted sesame seeds if desired.

# STEAMED GLUTINOUS RICE WITH BANANA

*Khao Tom Phad* (Makes about 16)

¼ cup dried black beans, to
  yield 1 cup cooked beans
16 pieces banana leaf or thick
  foil, 18 cm (7 in) square
¼ cup (2 oz) white sugar
½ teaspoon salt
1 cup (8 fl oz) coconut milk
1 cup white glutinous rice,
  washed and soaked
  overnight
3 bananas, sliced

1  Wash the black beans to remove any dust, then cover with water and bring to the boil. Put the lid on the pan, turn off the heat, and leave to stand. After 1 hour, return to the heat and simmer for 30–40 minutes, or until tender. (Leftover beans may be frozen for future use.)

2  Strip the banana leaves from their mid-ribs and wash them well. Cut into 18 cm (7 in) pieces and, holding each piece with tongs, pass them briefly over a gas flame to make them pliable. Whether using banana leaves or foil, make a small pleat 1.25 cm (½ in) wide down the centre of each piece to allow for the rice swelling during cooking.

3  Mix the sugar and salt with the coconut milk, add the drained rice and stir over moderate heat until the coconut milk is absorbed. The rice will still be only partially cooked.

4  Place 1 tablespoon of rice in the centre of each piece of leaf or foil. Cover with a piece of sliced banana and top with another tablespoon of rice. Press 6 black beans into the rice. Wrap and tie the leaf or fasten the folded ends with wooden toothpicks. If using foil, make a narrow double fold over the top of the rice and fold in the ends to seal. Repeat until all the rice is used up. Steam over boiling water for 45–50 minutes.

# COCONUT ICE-CREAM

*I-Tim Kati* (Serves 6)

*When I think of coconut ice-cream, I am whisked back in time to a memorable evening at the famous Oriental Hotel in Bangkok. Under a full moon, the* Loy Krathong *festival was celebrated with tableaux and Thai classical dancing and much festivity. At the end of an incredible buffet meal, the chef appeared with coconut ice-cream so fresh it was still in its churn, and served it to the appreciative guests.*

1 × 400 ml (13 fl oz) can
   coconut milk
100 ml (3½ fl oz) sweetened
   condensed milk
¾ cup (6 fl oz) water
⅓ cup (3 oz) white sugar
1½ teaspoons gelatine powder
¼ cup (2 fl oz) cold water

NOTE *Another very effective way to smooth out ice crystals when making ice-cream without a churn is to let the mixture freeze solid, then break it up into chunks and purée in a food processor until smooth. Return to the tray and refreeze.*

1 Combine the coconut milk and condensed milk in a bowl. Put the water and sugar in a small saucepan and heat gently, stirring until the sugar dissolves.

2 Sprinkle the gelatine over the ¼ cup cold water and leave to soften for a few minutes, then stir into the hot syrup. Cool the syrup, add to the coconut milk mixture and freeze the mixture in an ice-cream churn.

3 Alternatively, freeze in a shallow tray and when it is frozen around the edges but still slushy in the centre, turn out into a chilled bowl and whisk until smooth but not melted. Return it to the tray and freeze until firm. Leave at room temperature for a few minutes before serving. Decorate with shreds of toasted coconut or with very fine strips of agar-agar jelly (*page 186*). To make agar-agar jelly strips, pour some liquid jelly on a dinner plate to form a shallow layer. When set, cut with a sharp knife.

# MANGOES WITH SWEET RICE

*Khao Niew Ma Muang* (Serves 6)

*At a certain time of the year, this combination is all the rage in Thailand. It doesn't last long, because the rice has to be young and green, and mangoes of a certain variety. When green rice is not available, sticky or glutinous rice (also known as sweet rice) is used. The green colour and special flavour of the rice comes from* bai toey, *Thai for* pandanus *leaves. They are often available fresh, but the essence or paste is more convenient to use. The Malaysian name* pandan *is the only one usually featured on the bottle. It is readily available from Asian food stores. See colour plate on page 184.*

1 cup white glutinous rice
¾ cup (6 fl oz) thick coconut
 milk
pinch of salt
1 tablespoon white sugar
2 or 3 drops *pandan* essence
3 ripe mangoes

**1** Soak the rice overnight with sufficient water to cover. Drain off the water and place the rice in a heatproof bowl. Stir in the coconut milk, salt, sugar and essence. Place the bowl on a trivet in a pressure cooker with about 5 cm (2 in) water in the pan. Bring to pressure and cook at half pressure for 30 minutes.

**2** If a pressure cooker is not available, use a large steamer, steaming for 45 minutes to 1 hour, or until the rice is very tender and all the coconut milk absorbed. Leave to cool slightly.

**3** Take spoonfuls of the green-tinted rice and press into lightly oiled moulds, then release with a sharp tap on a hard surface; or use an ice-cream scoop.

**4** To slice mangoes, use a well sharpened stainless steel knife. I always cut off a small slice from the stem end because the sap found there is very irritating to sensitive throats. If the fruit is firm, peel it with a sharp knife and cut off the flesh in thick slices, one on either side of the seed. If completely ripe, as it should be, it is easier to peel by simply pulling off the skin in strips, starting at the top where the stem end has been removed. Arrange beside the rice. A simple leaf-vein carving on each mango is attractive. Serve at room temperature as the flavour of mango and texture of sticky rice are best when not chilled.

# MOCK BEAN PODS

*Khanom Tuay Paep* (Makes about 24)

**DOUGH**
1½ cups glutinous rice flour
½ cup (4 fl oz) boiling water

**FILLING**
½ cup dried mung beans
  without skin
1 tablespoon white sugar
2 tablespoons finely grated
  coconut
½ teaspoon salt

**COATING**
¼ cup crushed, toasted sesame
  seeds
¼ cup (2 oz) castor (superfine)
  sugar
1½ cups finely grated fresh
  coconut

**1 TO MAKE THE DOUGH,** sift the flour into a bowl and gradually add the water to form a soft dough. When cool enough to handle knead until smooth. Divide the dough in half and roll each piece into a cylinder 2.5 cm (1 in) in diameter, then cut into 2.5 cm (1 in) slices. Keep the working surface dusted with extra glutinous rice flour and roll each piece into a ball. Cover these with a dry cloth and set aside.

**2 TO MAKE THE FILLING,** cook the beans in boiling water to cover for about 10 minutes or until they are soft but not broken. Drain well, add the sugar and stir over low heat for 5–10 minutes longer. Mash lightly and mix with the grated coconut and salt.

**3** With floured fingers, flatten each ball of dough to a circle 6 cm (2½ in) in diameter and place 1 teaspoonful of filling in the centre. Pinch the edges together firmly, then soften the pinched edge and round it off to look like a seed pod. Continue with the remaining dough and filling.

**4** Drop the 'pods' into boiling water and when they float to the surface, lift out with a slotted spoon and drain.

**5 TO MAKE THE COATING,** combine the sesame seeds and sugar together. Toss the pods in the grated coconut and sprinkle liberally with the sugar mixture. Do not refrigerate, and serve on the same day.

# STICKY RICE BALLS IN FRESH COCONUT

*Khao Niew Kluk Maprao (Serves 6)*

*Many Thai sweets are based on glutinous rice which clings together most conveniently. Here the rice is flavoured and coloured before cooking, then rolled into oval shapes and coated with fresh coconut.*

2 cups white glutinous rice
1½ cups (12 fl oz) thick
   coconut milk
3 pinches of salt
3 tablespoons white sugar
red and green food colouring
2 or 3 drops each *pandan* (*bai
   toey*), rose and jasmine
   essences
about 1 cup grated fresh
   coconut

1 Soak the rice overnight with sufficient water to cover. Drain off the water and divide the rice and coconut milk equally into 3 heatproof bowls. Stir a pinch of salt and tablespoon of sugar into each bowl.

2 To one bowl add a drop or two of green food colouring and the *pandan* essence. To the second, add a drop or two of red food colouring – just enough to give a pale pink shade – and flavour with rose essence. To the third bowl add some jasmine essence.

3 Place the bowls in a steamer over hot water and bring to the boil. Cover and steam for 45 minutes to 1 hour, until the rice is tender and the coconut milk is absorbed.

4 Leave to cool slightly, then take spoonfuls of rice and roll into even-sized balls or ovals. Roll in grated fresh coconut and arrange on a plate. These snacks should not be refrigerated, but eaten on the same day.

# BLACK STICKY RICE

*Khao Niew Dum (Serves 4)*

*The best results, I feel, are obtained when the rice is soaked overnight, then steamed in a pressure cooker or steamer.*

1 cup black glutinous rice
¼ teaspoon salt
2 tablespoons sesame seeds,
   toasted
extra ½ teaspoon sea salt
1 cup freshly grated coconut
4 tablespoons palm sugar or
   dark brown sugar

1 Wash the rice well and soak overnight in cold water. Drain the rice and place in a heatproof bowl with ¾ cup (6 fl oz) of the soaking water and the ¼ teaspoon salt. Steam as directed in Mangoes with Sweet Rice (*page 191*).

2 Bruise the toasted sesame seeds lightly in a mortar together with the sea salt. Serve the rice warm or at room temperature, accompanied by the coconut, sesame seeds and palm sugar.

# TWO-LAYER PUMPKIN PUDDINGS

*Khanom Tuay* (Makes about 15)

**PUMPKIN LAYER**
1 cup cooked, mashed
    pumpkin
1 cup tapioca flour
¼ cup (2 oz) white sugar
¼ cup (2 fl oz) water

**COCONUT LAYER**
½ cup (4 fl oz) thick coconut
    milk
1 teaspoon rice flour
¼ teaspoon salt

1 **FOR THE PUMPKIN LAYER**, combine all the ingredients in a bowl and mix well until the sugar dissolves. Lightly oil small china cups (wine cups or other similar sized heatproof cups), with vegetable oil and fill to three-quarters full with the pumpkin mixture. Place in a steamer and steam over boiling water for 20 minutes.

2 Turn off the heat but do not remove the cups from the steamer. Mix together the coconut layer ingredients, and pour a teaspoon over the top of each pudding. Add more water to the steamer if necessary and steam for a further 10 minutes.

3 Cool, then run a knife around the edge, unmould and serve at room temperature. Do not chill.

# STEAMED PUMPKIN PUDDING

*Khanom Fug Tong* (Makes about 25 pieces)

500 g (1 lb) pumpkin, cooked
    and mashed
1¼ cups (10 fl oz) coconut
    milk
¾ cup (6 oz) white sugar
½ teaspoon jasmine essence
1 cup (4 oz) rice flour
¼ cup tapioca flour
¾ teaspoon salt
1 cup freshly grated coconut
extra grated coconut mixed
    with a pinch of salt
    (optional)

1 Lightly brush a 20 cm (8 in) square or round tin with oil. Sieve the pumpkin or purée in a food processor.

2 Warm the coconut milk and stir in the sugar until dissolved. Combine the coconut milk and pumpkin, and flavour with jasmine essence.

3 Sift both flours and ½ teaspoon of the salt into a bowl, then mix in the pumpkin mixture and ½ cup of the grated coconut. Pour into the prepared tin and sprinkle with the remaining coconut mixed with the remaining ¼ teaspoon salt.

4 Place the tin in a steamer and steam over fast boiling water for 30–35 minutes, or until firm. Allow to cool, then cut into squares or diamond shapes with a wet knife. Sprinkle with additional lightly salted coconut if desired.

# GREEN AND GOLD LAYERED PUDDING

*Khanom Chaun Tua* (Makes about 30 pieces)

*The gold layer is made with mung bean paste, sweetened and flavoured with coconut milk, while the clear green layer is tapioca starch. They are poured into a pan and steamed in layers and the final result is a pretty ribbon effect of contrasting colours and textures.*

**GOLD LAYER**
½ **cup split and skinned mung beans**
½ **cup (4 oz) white sugar**
1 **cup (8 fl oz) coconut milk**
¼ **teaspoon jasmine essence**
¼ **teaspoon yellow food colouring**
½ **cup glutinous rice flour**
¼ **cup tapioca flour**

**GREEN LAYER**
½ **cup tapioca flour**
2 **tablespoons glutinous rice flour**
1 **cup (8 fl oz) water**
⅓ **cup (3 oz) white sugar**
½ **teaspoon *pandan* (*bai toey*) paste or essence (for colour and flavour) or green food colouring**

1 **TO MAKE THE GOLD LAYER**, wash the mung beans and put them into a small pan with enough water to cover. Boil gently for about 15–20 minutes, or until they are very soft, then drain off any water that has not been absorbed. Mash with a fork or potato masher until smooth.

2 Add the sugar and coconut milk and mix well, then stir in the jasmine essence, yellow food colouring, rice flour and tapioca flour.

3 **TO MAKE THE GREEN LAYER**, mix together both flours, water and sugar. Colour a deep green and flavour with *pandan* paste or essence.

4 Spray a 20–23 cm (8–9 in) round or square pan with non-stick food spray, or brush lightly with oil. Pour in one-third of the gold mixture, cover and steam for 5–8 minutes over boiling water until set.

5 Pour half the green mixture over the first layer, cover and steam for 10 minutes, or until firm. There may be a little liquid on the surface, so pick up the pan using a tea towel or heatproof mitts and pour it off.

6 Gently ladle another third of the gold mixture over the green layer, add more boiling water if necesary, and steam a further 5–8 minutes until firm. Repeat with the remaining green mixture, and finally the last of the gold mixture. Steam for 10 minutes, then leave to become quite cold. Cut into strips, squares or diamond shapes to serve. This sweet may be made ahead and kept refrigerated for a few days.

# THREE-COLOURED SWEET RICE BALLS

*Bua Loy Sarm See* (Serves 6–8)

*When in Thailand researching this book, one of my priorities was to learn how to make the fascinating sweets. I could hardly believe my eyes when I found out that each of the tiny little balls of rice flour in this dessert is moulded by hand! Yet, if two or three friends sit together and the talk is entertaining, it is done in half an hour, most pleasantly.*

**YELLOW MIXTURE**
1 cup glutinous rice flour
1 cup steamed, mashed
 pumpkin

**WHITE MIXTURE**
1 cup glutinous rice flour
1 cup cooked, mashed and
 sieved potato or taro

**GREEN MIXTURE**
1 cup glutinous rice flour
*pandan* (*bai toey*) leaves or
 essence

**COCONUT SYRUP**
2 cups (16 fl oz) coconut milk
½ cup (4 oz) white sugar or to
 taste
¼ teaspoon salt

---

**NOTE** *If only a small amount of dessert is needed, halve these quantities. You can, in fact, use half the white mixture, flavoured and coloured a delicate green with pandan essence to replace the full quantity of green mixture.*

---

1 In three separate bowls make up mixtures of the rice flour with the mashed vegetables and, in the case of the green mixture, with sufficient water to moisten and make a firm dough. Add a few drops of cold water if the mixtures are too stiff; a little extra rice flour if too soft to hold their shape when moulded.

2 Take tiny bits of the dough and form smooth balls, keeping each colour separate. Bring a pan of water to the boil and cook one colour at a time, simmering, until they come to the surface. Lift out on a slotted spoon and put into separate bowls of ice water.

3 Combine the coconut syrup ingredients in a saucepan and stir while bringing to the boil. Remove from the heat and cool until just warm. For each serving, place ½ cup of the rice balls, in a mixture of colours, in each bowl with enough syrup to cover and serve warm or at room temperature.

# CARAMEL CUPS

*Khanom Tuay Fug Tong (Makes about 36)*

*The little cups used for steaming these and other sweets are generally found in Asian stores where Thai and Vietnamese goods are sold, and are quite inexpensive.*

¾ cup (6 oz) palm sugar
¾ cup (6 fl oz) water
1 cup (4 oz) rice flour
3 tablespoons arrowroot
2½ cups (20 fl oz) thick
    coconut milk

**TOPPING**
¼ cup (2 fl oz) thick coconut
    milk
1 teaspoon rice flour
¼ teaspoon salt

1 Caramelise the palm sugar to a dark brown colour in a wok or heavy saucepan, stirring constantly to prevent burning. Remove from the heat and add the water to dissolve the caramel. Cool and strain the syrup.

2 Combine the rice flour and arrowroot with ¾ cup (6 fl oz) of the coconut milk. Beat well until smooth, then add the remaining coconut milk. Gradually beat in the caramel syrup.

3 Heat ungreased china cups for 10 minutes in a steamer and fill with the caramel mixture. Steam for 25 minutes or until firm.

4 Make the topping by heating the coconut milk, rice flour and salt in a small saucepan, stirring, until it boils and thickens. Allow to cool. When the caramel cups are at room temperature, pipe on small rosettes of coconut topping to decorate. They may be served in the cups or turned out onto plates.

# DIMPLED CUPS

*Khanom Nam Dog Mai (Makes about 18)*

1 cup (4 oz) rice flour
1 tablespoon arrowroot
½ cup (4 oz) white sugar
2 cups (16 fl oz) water,
    flavoured with jasmine
green and red food colouring

1 Combine the rice flour and arrowroot. Heat the sugar and 1 cup (8 fl oz) of the water together in a pan, stirring to dissolve the sugar. Mix into the flour and knead well until smooth. Gradually add the remaining cup of water.

2 Place small china cups in a steamer and steam for 10 minutes to heat. Divide the mixture in half and add a drop or two of green or red food colouring to each. While the cups are hot, fill them to three-quarters full with the mixture and steam for 20–25 minutes over boiling water, until the surface is dimpled and firm. Unmould and serve warm or at room temperature with the dimple uppermost.

# 'FORGET TO SWALLOW'

*Khanom Lüm Klün* (Makes about 24)

*This is the literal translation of the Thai name for these simple but delicious sweets, translucent, and so tender that they slip down without any effort.*

2 tablespoons mung bean
    flour
2 cups (16 fl oz) water
¾ cup (6 oz) white sugar
jasmine essence
food colouring (optional)

TOPPING
¼ cup (2 fl oz) coconut milk
1 teaspoon rice flour
pinch of salt

1 Combine the mung bean flour, water and sugar in a saucepan, stirring until the flour is incorporated. Place over medium heat and bring to the boil, stirring constantly. If you like, divide the mixture in two or three portions and colour each one a delicate shade with one or two drops of food colouring.

2 Have ready little foil or waxed paper confectionery cups or, if possible, small square boxes made from fresh *pandan* (*bai toey*) leaves. Pour a little of the mixture into each cup and leave to set.

3 Heat the topping ingredients together until it boils and thickens, then leave to cool. Put into a piping bag fitted with a star or flower nozzle, and pipe a tiny rosette onto each sweet. The slightly salty taste of the coconut contrasts delightfully with the sweets.

# BASIL SEEDS IN COCONUT SYRUP

*Med Manglak Nam Kati* (Serves 4)

2 tablespoons basil seeds
    (*manglak*)
2 cups (16 fl oz) coconut milk
½ cup (4 oz) white sugar
½ cup glutinous rice flour
blue food colouring
1 few drops jasmine or rose
    essence

1 Soak the basil seeds in a bowl of water for 10 minutes until each black seed develops a jelly-like translucent coating. Warm the coconut milk and stir in the sugar until it dissolves.

2 Mix the rice flour with just enough cold water to give a moulding consistency and work in a drop or two of blue food colouring to give a delicate shade. Take small pieces and roll between the palms to make little 'snake' shapes. Drop into a pan of boiling water and when they float to the top, lift them out on a slotted spoon and immerse in a bowl of ice water.

3 Just before serving combine the soaked seeds and the coconut milk. Drain the blue rice flour shapes and stir in. If you like, add a little crushed ice.

# LAYERED SWEET

*Khanom Chaun* (Makes 45 or more pieces, depending on size)

*Pandan paste can be obtained from Asian food stores.* Khanom Chaun *flour is a mixture of rice and tapioca flours (page 208).*

¾ cup (3 oz) rice flour
185 g (6 oz) *khanom chaun* flour
280 g (9 oz) white sugar
1 × 400 ml (13 fl oz) can coconut milk
½ teaspoon salt
3 cups (24 fl oz) water
*pandan* (*bai toey*) paste

1  Mix all the ingredients together, stirring gently, until smooth. Strain through a fine sieve. Take out 1 cup (8 fl oz) of the batter and set aside. Divide the remainder into 2 equal portions. Colour one of these light green with the *pandan* paste. Leave the other portion white.

2  Spray a 23 cm (9 in) square tin with non-stick spray or brush it lightly with oil. Place on a rack over hot water in an electric frypan or steamer, cover and bring to the boil (set the frypan at 200°C/400°F).

3  Pour in a thin layer (about a scant cupful) of light green batter and steam for 5 minutes, or until set. Pour over the same amount of white batter and steam for 5 minutes.

4  Continue in this way until the batter is used up, except for the cupful of batter that was set aside. Colour this a deep green with *pandan* paste and pour over the other layers. Steam the final layer for 15 minutes. Cool and cut into squares. Do not refrigerate, and serve these the same day.

5  For a variation, colour one portion pale pink and the other pale green. Save a cupful of caramel mixture (*page 197*). Make several thin layers of each mixture and cook as above.

# WATER CHESTNUT SWEET

*Tuptim Grob (Serves 4)*

Tuptim *means 'rubies', and it is also the word for pomegranate;* grob *means 'crisp, crunchy'. A descriptive name for this simple dessert based on little pieces of water chestnuts with a glistening, transparent coating of tapioca flour. Fresh coconut milk is really superior to canned coconut milk in desserts, and should be used if fresh coconuts are available.*

¾ cup (6 oz) white sugar
¾ cup (6 fl oz) water
200 g (7 oz) water chestnuts,
    fresh or canned
red and green food colouring
rosewater or jasmine essence
a few drops *pandan* essence
about ¾ cup (5 oz) tapioca
    flour
1 cup (8 fl oz) fresh coconut
    milk
⅛ teaspoon salt
crushed ice

1 Make a syrup with the sugar and water, stirring over heat until the sugar dissolves. Cool.

2 Drain the canned water chestnuts, rinse in cold water, then cut each one into about 8 pieces, roughly equal in size. If fresh water chestnuts are available, peel, dice and boil them for 10 minutes.

3 Pour ½ cup (4 fl oz) of the sugar water into each of two white bowls. Add red food colouring and a few drops of rose or jasmine essence to one, and green food colouring and *pandan* essence to the other. Make the colours fairly strong. Add half the diced water chestnuts to one bowl and half to the other, stir and leave to soak for 10 minutes.

4 Divide the tapioca flour between two sheets of greaseproof (non-stick baking) paper. Drain the soaking water chestnuts if they have absorbed a fair amount of colour, otherwise leave them longer. Keeping the two colours separate, roll the chestnuts in the tapioca flour until well coated.

5 Bring a saucepan of water to the boil. Gently shake the red-tinted water chestnuts in a strainer, or toss from hand to hand so excess flour comes away. Drop into the boiling water and allow to cook until the pieces rise to the surface. Drain and plunge immediately into ice water.

6 Using fresh boiling water, repeat the procedure with the green-tinted chestnuts, and cool them in a separate bowl of ice water.

7 To serve, pour a quarter of the syrup into a tall glass and carefully place some green, then some red-tinted chestnuts in the glass, keeping the layers separate. Gently spoon over some of the coconut milk mixed with the salt, and add crushed ice, or serve in bowls.

# STEAMED CUSTARD IN PUMPKIN SHELL

*Sankaya Fug Tong (Serves 4–6)*

*The sweetness of pumpkin goes well with the flavour of palm sugar. If you have difficulty buying palm sugar, use brown sugar.*

200 g (6½ oz) palm sugar
¼ cup (2 fl oz) water
1¼ cups (10 fl oz) canned
   coconut cream
3 whole eggs
2 egg yolks
⅛ teaspoon salt
a few drops rosewater or rose
   essence
4–6 small golden nugget
   pumpkins or 1 medium-
   sized pumpkin

---

NOTE *If using one medium-to-large pumpkin instead of individual ones, cut the dessert into wedges so each person gets a slice of pumpkin with the firm custard inside.*

---

1  Put the palm sugar into a small saucepan with the water. Heat gently until melted. Remove from the heat and mix with the coconut cream.

2  Beat the eggs and egg yolks together and add to the coconut milk mixture. Flavour with the salt and rosewater. Strain into a jug.

3  Cut off the top of each pumpkin and set aside. Scoop out all the seeds and membranes and place the pumpkins in a large steamer or on a rack in a large pan over hot water.

4  Fill with the custard and steam over gently boiling water for 20 minutes, or until the custard is set and a knife inserted in the centre comes out clean. Set the lids alongside the pumpkins when steaming to cook them. Allow to cool, then chill. Place a lid on each pumpkin before serving.

# TAPIOCA WITH SWEET CORN AND YOUNG COCONUT

*Saku, Khao Poad, Maprao Orn* (Serves 4)

*Those who have encountered young coconut in lands where it grows will know that the flesh of an immature nut is quite different from the hard white meat of a mature coconut. At this stage of development the meat is soft and sweet. Translucent at first, it becomes slightly milky in appearance, yet is soft enough to spoon from the shell. Young coconut is now available either frozen or in cans.*

½ cup (3 oz) tapioca
¾ cup (6 fl oz) water
3 tablespoons white sugar
½ cup sweet corn kernels
½ cup young coconut, cut
    into squares or diamond
    shapes

1 Cook, drain and rinse the tapioca as described in Bananas in Coconut Cream (*page 188*).

2 Make a syrup by boiling the water and sugar together for 3 minutes. Add the corn kernels and simmer gently for about 10 minutes, adding more water if the syrup boils down and becomes thick – this should be a light syrup. Cool to room temperature.

3 Combine the tapioca and syrup, then stir in the young coconut. Divide into 4 bowls and serve warm.

# MINIATURE MOULDED FRUITS

## Lug Chup

*The Thai name for these tiny fruits is* Lug Chup *('u' as in 'put'), which translates as 'small magic'. They are made with mung bean paste, the Asian substitute for marzipan. It has a similar texture, but is usually flavoured with coconut milk and floral essences and keeps well in the refrigerator for at least a week. Buy the skinned and split beans, not the whole mung beans in their green skins.*

1½ cups split mung beans
1 cup (8 oz) white sugar
½ cup (4 fl oz) thick coconut
    milk
a few drops jasmine essence
food colouring

**GLAZING AND FINISHING**
3 teaspoons agar-agar powder
2 cups (16 fl oz) water
calyxes and stems from fresh
    chillies and strawberries

**NOTE** *An alternative glaze can be made with 2 tablespoons gelatine dissolved in 2 cups (16 fl oz) water. Sprinkle the gelatine over 1 cup (8 fl oz) water and leave to soak for 5 minutes. Dissolve it either in a microwave oven on high for 35–40 seconds or by standing the cup in a small pan of simmering water on the stove. When the gelatine is dissolved allow it to cool to room temperature and stir in the remaining cup of water, which should be at the same temperature. This solution will not set as readily, and will not need to be melted as many times.*

1 Wash the beans and soak in plenty of cold water. Drain and rinse. Put them into a saucepan with just enough water to cover and cook with a lid on the pan until the beans are soft enough to mash easily between the fingers. Drain away any remaining water.

2 Mash the beans until smooth and return to the pan (use a heavy-based pan) with the sugar and coconut milk. Cook over medium heat, stirring constantly, for about 30 minutes. Lower the heat as the mixture becomes drier and be careful not to let the paste catch on the base of the pan. When ready it should be very smooth and of a moulding consistency.

3 Remove from the heat and when cool mix in the jasmine essence. Alternatively, store the moulded and painted fruits overnight in a container with some jasmine blossoms or a scented candle to impart a faint perfume.

4 Take half-teaspoons of the mixture and roll into smooth balls, then mould each one to represent a fruit or vegetable. Insert a fine toothpick in the stem end of each fruit, then paint them with food colouring and stick the other end into a block of polystyrene while they dry.

5 **TO GLAZE THE FRUITS**, stir the agar-agar powder into the water and heat gently until it is completely dissolved. Allow to cool slightly before dipping the fruits. It may be necessary to reheat the agar-agar gently to keep it at a liquid consistency.

6 Dip each fruit in the glaze and leave to dry on the toothpick. When all the fruit have been dipped, dip the earlier ones a second time. When all the fruits are quite dry and no longer sticky to the touch, remove the toothpicks. Insert tiny leaves made by trimming to size twigs of murraya or other non-toxic plant varieties. Calyxes from fresh chillies or strawberries can be used to give a life-like appearance to the moulded fruits. Serve as part of a selection of sweets.

# PRONUNCIATION GUIDE

You don't have to speak Thai to enjoy the flavours of Thailand, but it helps if one can recognise famous dishes when they are called only by their Thai names. Some are so well known that even *farang* (foreigners) would not dream of ordering anything other than *Mee Grob* or *Tom Yum Goong*. But if you expect even the simplest name to be spelled the same way on every menu, you will surely be disappointed.

The letters K and G seem to be interchangeable, so are L and R. *Kaeng* or *gaeng* are the same, and rhyme with *gang* – sort of. Chicken is *gai* or *kai* (rhymes with 'sky'), but I am told that *kai* also means 'egg'. So, arbitrarily perhaps, I have used *gai* for chicken, *kai* for egg.

Prawns are *kung* or *goong*, but the vowel(s) are like the 'u' in 'put', even if to the Anglo-Saxon eye it seems reasonable that *kung* should rhyme with *hung*. Thus, *Lug Chup* ('look choop') testifies to the validity of that rule, but in a *yum* (salad), it is 'u' as in 'hut'. We didn't use *yam* because there would be the temptation to pronounce it like a sweet potato!

To prevent similar understandable errors, my Thai friend, Rachnee (Dang) Howarth, spent hours translating recipe titles, with phonetic spelling so they could be pronounced correctly by enthusiasts who cannot speak Thai. I am immensely grateful to her. Here are some ground rules.

A as in 'father' or the 'u' sound in 'but'.
AE rhymes with 'gang', but more drawn out.
AI rhymes with 'why'.
AO rhymes with 'cow'.
E as in 'pet'.
I as in 'pit'.
O as in 'or'.
U most often as in 'put', sometimes as in 'putt'.
G as in 'goat'.
J as in 'joke'.
CH as in 'chew'.
PH as in 'pet' (the two letters do not combine to give the 'f' sound).

# GLOSSARY

*Thanks to the popularity of Thai food worldwide, many food companies in Thailand are exporting an excellent range of spices, sauces, herbs, and other requisites. Ingredients are obviously best if used in their fresh form, but since not everybody has access to large Asian shopping centres, I have also listed other forms in which they are sold. Bear in mind that demand creates supply, so keep asking your local supplier for what you need.*

**agar-agar**   *woon*
A setting agent refined from seaweed, sometimes known as vegetable gelatine. It sets and stays solid without refrigeration and is ideal for use in warm climates. Available in powder form or strands at Asian grocery stores, some health food stores and chemists. Gelatine is not really a suitable substitute as the texture will be totally different and it will take twice as much gelatine powder to set the given amount of liquid.

**aubergine**   *see* eggplant

**basil**   *horapa; manglak; krapow*
An important fresh herb in Thai cooking. Dried basil would be a poor substitute. Since basil is easily grown, it is worth keeping a few plants of sweet basil in a pot or window box.

*Horapa* is the most commonly used and is equivalent to the large-leaf sweet basil (*Ocimum basilicum*) usual in European cooking.

The smaller leaf of *manglak* (*Ocimum canum*) is more pungent and lemon scented, and its seeds (*luk manglak*) are used in desserts and drinks. They are supposed to have a cooling effect on the body, and are used as a medicine for stomach ailments. When dry they are tiny, oval and brownish-black. When soaked in cold water for a few minutes, they develop a slippery, translucent coat around the seed, which is why they are sometimes called 'frog's eggs'.

*Krapow* (*Ocimum sanctum*) is used only in curries. Its leaves are tinged with red.

**bean curd**   *tao hu*
Made from soybeans, bean curd or tofu takes many forms. There is the soft, fresh bean curd used in soups and other dishes, usually sold in a container with water which should be changed daily for the 2 or 3 days it will keep in the refrigerator. If you wish to keep bean curd for some time, buy Japanese tofu in sealed packages, which keeps for months without refrigeration. After opening, store in the refrigerator and use within 2 days. Freezing is not recommended.

Pressed or *firm bean curd* is sold in blocks, wrapped in plastic film. It is used in fried dishes and is less likely to disintegrate during cooking. It generally does not keep for long, so use it fairly promptly or it will discolour and develop a slimy surface and sour smell.

Fermented or *red bean curd* is sold in jars. It keeps well and imparts a salty, pungent flavour.

*Bean curd skin* is sold as dried, flat sheets. Soak in warm water until flexible before using.

**bean starch vermicelli**   *see* noodles, transparent

**bitter gourd**   *ma ra*
A gourd (*Momordica charantia*) with a distinctive bitter flavour – an acquired taste. It resembles a green cucumber pointed at the tip with a glossy, pebbly-textured skin. Dark green when immature, it turns golden with red seeds when ripe. Use it when it is apple-green and the seeds are still pale and tender. No substitute.

**black fungus**   *hed hunu*
Also known as 'jelly mushrooms' or 'cloud ear fungus', black fungus (*Auricularia polytricha*) is sold in dried form and resembles greyish-black bits of torn paper. When soaked in water for 10 minutes it swells to translucent, jelly-like

brown shapes. Having no flavour of its own, it is used for its resilient texture and testifies to the Chinese influence in Thai cooking. It may be omitted without affecting the dish.

**black sticky rice**   *see* rice

**cardamom**   *luk kravan*
This fragrant spice (*Elettaria cardamomum*) is not typically found in Thai dishes. It is an important part of Masaman curry, which is an Indian-influenced Thai dish.

**cha plu**
Cha plu (*Piper sarmentosum*) is a creeper belonging to the pepper family. It has glossy green leaves with a spiciness reminiscent of betel leaves, and is used to enclose little snacks so it forms an edible wrapping. Substitute soft lettuce or tender spinach leaves.

**chillies**   *prik*
Chillies (*Capsicum frutescens*) come in all sizes and a variety of shapes and colours. Fresh chillies used in Thai cooking are usually the small, hot ones. As a general rule, large chillies are milder and the tiny ones are devilishly hot. Colour is no indication. If very hot food is not to your taste, use larger chillies for flavour without excessive heat.

When handling chillies, wear gloves and take care not to handle the cut surfaces. Wash your hands in cold water as soon as you finish, rubbing well with bicarbonate of soda (baking soda) to soothe the burning sensation. I find that holding the chilli by its stem and taking care to avoid the volatile oils is well worth the trouble. PLEASE don't touch your eyes with hands which have recently touched chillies, and be mindful of touching children. Plastic gloves are a wise precaution.

If you like a hot curry, leave the seeds but if you prefer less heat, remove them.

Dried chillies are safer to handle, but wash your hands well afterwards. To use, snip off the stems of dried chillies and shake out the seeds, snip or break the chillies into pieces and soak in hot water for 15 minutes to soften. Dried chillies are also sold as coarse flakes or fine powder. Flakes are more often used in Thai food.

**cinnamon**   *ob chuey*
Cinnamon (*Cinnamomum zeylanicum*) is not much used in Thai food except in dishes with an Indian influence, such as Masaman curry. You can distinguish true cinnamon by the thin, pale bark which is sun-dried to form quills packed one inside the other. Buy the quills because most of what is sold as ground cinnamon is actually ground cassia – similar in flavour, but much stronger and lacking the delicacy of true cinnamon.

**coconut milk and cream**
Not many writers now refer to the clear liquid inside a coconut as 'coconut milk'. This used to be a common misconception among Western food writers. Most people now know that coconut milk is the rich white liquid extracted from the *flesh* of mature coconuts. As recently as a few months ago, however, viewers in many countries were exposed to the badly researched commentary of a television cooking show presenter who continually referred to the clear liquid inside the nut as 'coconut milk'. Just as I thought it was safe not to labour the point, it has become necessary to disabuse people of the notion once more.

If you can purchase good quality unsweetened coconut milk in cans or tetra packs, do so. Many western supermarkets now stock coconut milk and there are several excellent brands.

Where *coconut cream* or *thick coconut milk* is called for, use it straight from the can without diluting.

For *coconut milk*, mix equal parts of canned coconut milk and water. For *thin coconut milk*, dilute one part canned coconut milk with two parts water.

For curries and other savoury dishes, I would not hesitate to use either canned coconut milk or instant dried coconut milk powder. Choose a brand that contains no sugar, is white rather than grey in appearance, and smooth rather than clotted. Coconut milk is very perishable and if not using all the same day, freeze in ice-cube trays. When solid, pop them into a freezer bag – handy if you want to add a tablespoon or two of coconut milk to enrich a soup or sauce.

Reconstitute instant dried coconut milk powder according to the directions on the label. Taste, and if necessary use more powder to give a richer result.

If canned or instant coconut milk is not readily available where you shop, prepare it by using either fresh or desiccated coconut.

While thankful for the convenience of these products, certain desserts do need the incomparable flavour of fresh coconut milk that has not been treated by extreme heat. To make fresh coconut milk, choose a coconut that is full of water, devoid of any dampness on the shell with no mould or moisture leaking through any of the three spots at one end. When opened, it should smell sweet and fresh.

To open a coconut, heft it in one hand and, wielding a hammer or the back of a cleaver with the other, tap firmly around the middle of the nut. When a deep crack appears, insert the corner of the cleaver blade and let the water run into a jug. (If the nut is very fresh, the water makes a nice drink.) A few more blows and it will break in two. If possible, grate the white portion right in the shell with a grater made expressly for coconut.

Pour 2 cups (16 fl oz) hot water over the grated flesh of one coconut and knead hard, then strain through a fine sieve, pressing out as much moisture as possible. This is the first extract or *thick milk*. Pour more water over the grated coconut and knead again to extract more milk. Strain. This is *thin milk*. Repeat. Unless thick coconut milk is specified, use a combination of thick and thin milk in most recipes.

If a recipe calls for *coconut cream*, use the rich layer that forms on top of the first extract after it has been left in the refrigerator for an hour or so.

If fresh coconuts are not available, use desiccated coconut or shredded unsweetened coconut. Put 2 cups (16 fl oz) desiccated coconut in a bowl and pour 2½ cups (20 fl oz) hot water over it. Allow to cool to lukewarm. Knead firmly for a few minutes and strain through a fine strainer or muslin, pressing out as much liquid as possible. This should yield about 1½ cups (12 fl oz) *thick coconut milk*.

Repeat the process, using the same coconut and another 2½ cups (20 fl oz) hot water. Because of the moisture retained in the coconut, it should yield about 2 cups (16 fl oz) of *thin coconut milk*.

A blender or food processor makes kneading quicker and easier, but straining and pressing out the liquid must still be done. For a richer coconut milk, use hot milk instead of hot water.

### coriander (cilantro/Chinese parsley)
*pak chee*

Fresh coriander (*Coriandrum sativum*) is indispensable in Thai cooking. It is readily available in large fruit and vegetable markets, and most certainly in Asian stores. But if you don't live within reach of these facilities, it is not difficult to grow: all you need is a patch of earth and patience, since the seeds take from 18–21 days to germinate. Scatter the seeds, cover very lightly with soil and water regularly.

The distinctive, pungent flavour of coriander does not survive in dried form. If fresh coriander is not available, substitute fresh mint or fresh sweet basil. The flavour will be different, but is preferable to dried coriander leaves.

Coriander seeds, on the other hand, are used dried. They are sold whole or ground, and are a basic ingredient in curry pastes. The aroma and flavour are quite different to that of the fresh herb.

Peculiar to Thai cooking is the use of coriander roots. Many shops sell the plant without the roots, which is all right for Indian or Chinese food but lacks the vital flavour for Thai cooking. Wash the plants thoroughly, scrubbing the roots clean. Separate the lower part of the stems under a cold tap so that any sand is flushed away.

**cummin**  *yee ra*
An important component of curry pastes, cummin (*Cuminum cyminum*) may be bought as whole seeds or ground. Before using, roast the seeds lightly until fragrant. Pound finely or grind.

**dried shrimp**  *see* shrimp, dried

**eggplant**  *makua*
A very popular vegetable in Thailand, and there are many varieties used, from small, green and pea-sized to the large purple or white. In between there are eggplants about the size and shape of eggs (perhaps this is what led to its English name). The skins of some have a delicate green-and-white tracery, while others are in pretty mauve shades. These are sometimes eaten raw with a *Nam Prik* sauce.

**fish sauce**  *nam pla*
This thin, brown, salty sauce is made from a small variety of fish or from tiny shrimp which are layered with salt and left in the sun. The salty liquid drips through into a container, is bottled, and then left in the sun until it is clear and pale and has developed its characteristic smell. Mixed with lime juice or chillies, it is used as a condiment. An indispensable ingredient in Thai cooking.

**flour,** *khanom chaun*
A mixture of rice flour and tapioca flour, used in making sweetmeats. No substitute. It is sold in packets in Asian food stores.

**flour, mung bean**
This white starch becomes clear when boiled, and is used in desserts. Substitute arrowroot or cornflour (cornstarch).

**flour, rice**  *pang khao chao*
Most Western supermarkets carry ground rice or rice flour in packets, which is used to thicken sauces. Substitute cornflour (cornstarch) if necessary. *Glutinous rice flour (pank khao niew)* is used in desserts.

**flour, roasted rice**
It is possible to buy small packets of ready roasted rice flour or do it yourself (*page 118*). It is considered an essential part of some savoury recipes, but is not detectable to the untrained palate.

**flour, tapioca**  *pang mun*
A clear starch for making sweets.

**galangal (greater)**  *kha*
Greater galangal (*Alpinia galanga*) is a rhizome which looks similar to ginger and is sometimes called Siamese Ginger. Also labelled with its Indonesian name of *laos* or its Malaysian name, *lengkuas*. It is sold fresh, frozen, bottled in brine, sliced and dried, or dried and ground. Wherever possible use fresh, frozen or bottled galangal.

**galangal (lesser)**  *krachai*
The slender tubers of the lesser galangal (*Kaempferia pandurata*) grow in a bunch and look nothing at all like ginger. They are smaller but more strongly flavoured than greater galangal, and are used less frequently, mostly in fish dishes.

**garlic**  *kratiem*
Garlic (*Allium sativum*) is indispensable in Thai cooking, and is available everywhere in its fresh form. It is valued for its flavour and its health-giving properties as it controls high blood pressure, reduces cholesterol and is a natural antibiotic. Since garlic cloves vary greatly in size, I have given measurements in teaspoons of finely chopped or crushed garlic.

Dried garlic is sometimes available in granulated form, in thin slices or flakes. When *crisp-fried garlic* is needed, save time and effort by using dried garlic flakes. They cook very quickly and must not be allowed to brown or they will become bitter. Lift them quickly from the oil with a fine wire strainer. When fried and cooled, crush them for sprinkling over appetisers or salads.

*Pickled garlic (kratiem dong)* is another popular flavour accent in Thai dishes. Sold in jars in a light pickling mixture of vinegar, sugar and salt, it will keep indefinitely without refrigeration. Do not attempt to separate or peel the cloves, simply slice through the whole bulb.

### garlic chives  *ton kui chai*
Also known as Chinese chives (*Allium tuberosum*), these flat, thick leaves are served alongside noodle dishes, or cut into short lengths and added to the dish as required.

### ginger  *khing*
Whenever ginger (*Zingiber officinale*) is mentioned in Thai recipes, fresh ginger, not the dried, ground ginger is called for. The two are not interchangeable. To preserve fresh ginger it can be cut into pieces, wrapped in foil and frozen; peeled, divided into small pieces and packed in a well washed and dried bottle covered with dry sherry; puréed in a blender with just enough water and dry sherry to facilitate movement, then stored in a glass screwtop jar in the refrigerator. It will keep for a few weeks. Fresh minced ginger can also be bought in supermarkets.

The strength of ginger depends on how mature it is: try and get young, tender and pink-tipped ginger which doesn't need peeling. If it's mature and thick-skinned, scrape off the skin with a sharp knife. Chop finely or grate before measuring, discarding any tough fibres that collect on the grater.

### ginger, sweet red
Sold in bottles, these slices of ginger are preserved in sugar syrup, both syrup and ginger being coloured red.

### glutinous rice flour  *see flour, rice*

### Golden Mountain sauce  *poo kow tong*
This clear, brown, salty sauce looks like light soy sauce or fish sauce, but tastes like neither. The nearest equivalent is a Swiss product called Maggi Seasoning or, in Europe, Maggi Arome – a well-established product of which, I do believe, the Golden Mountain sauce is a copy. It is based on hydrolysed vegetable proteins and certainly gives a lift to flavours.

### jasmine  *mali*
The unopened flower buds of *Jasminum sambac* are picked in the cool of the evening and soaked in water overnight to impart their fragrance. This water is used for making sweets, sometimes for extracting the coconut milk to be used in desserts. Jasmine essence (labelled *mali*) is available, and probably more practical, if not quite as romantic.

### *krachai*  *see galangal, lesser*

### lemon grass  *takrai*
This hardy herb (*Cymbopogon citratus*) is easy to grow and may be purchased at many nurseries. It grows throughout Asia and also in Australia, Africa, South America and Florida in the United States. If planted in a well-drained, sunny spot it will multiply vigorously and you will always have a supply. Choose well-developed, thick stems and cut close to the root with a sharp knife. The leaves are not used in Thai cooking.

Stems of fresh lemon grass are readily available at Asian food stores. The whole stem may be simmered in curries or soups and removed before serving. The only part used in pastes, or sliced finely in salads, is the tender white portion just above the root. Discard the outer layer, wash well and cut into very thin slices with a sharp knife. This ensures there are no long fibres in the finished dishes.

If using strips of dried lemon grass, first reconstitute in hot water, or substitute 2 strips of lemon zest for each stem of lemon grass.

### lily buds
When you see a recipe using this ingredient, you may be sure it was originally Chinese. These slender golden buds are sold dried and should be soaked until soft before use. The flavour is very delicate and they may be omitted if they are difficult to find.

### lime  *ma nao*
Small deep-green limes (*Citrus aurantifolia*) used for both rind and juice. Substitute any limes in season, or lemons.

### lime, kaffir  *makrut*
The leaves and rind of this lumpy-skinned green lime (*Citrus hystrix*) add a special fragrance to Thai food.

Buy fresh lime leaves for the best flavour. They have double leaves in two distinct sections and a wonderful fragrance. If you cannot find these, use frozen or dried leaves, the latter needing to be soaked first in boiling water for 20 minutes. Or use fresh lime or lemon leaves if you have them growing, although they are not as fragrant as kaffir lime. Only the fresh leaf is suitable for garnish. I usually remove the centre ribs before shredding the leaves finely.

The rind of kaffir limes is also used for its intense citrus flavour and the best way to obtain this (unless you have access to fresh limes) is to buy frozen kaffir limes. Keep them in the freezer so they are very hard, then grate on the fine surface of a grater. Use only the coloured portion, not the white pith underneath. The rind is also sold dried, but because it has the white pith with it, I find it rather bitter. Use it if you like, but in small quantities. A suitable alternative is the rind of fresh Tahitian or West Indian limes.

### mung beans, split
It is possible to purchase split beans with their skins removed from Asian food stores. Used most frequently in desserts.

### mushrooms, shiitake   *hed hom*
Because they are dried and imported, these fragrant mushrooms are not cheap but they do add a distinctive flavour to Chinese-influenced Thai dishes. Do not substitute dried continental mushrooms, as the flavour is quite different.

### mushrooms, straw   *hed farng*
This cultivated mushroom (*Volvariella volvaceae*) consists of an edible sheath within which is the mushroom. If bought fresh the mushrooms should be blanched in boiling water for a few minutes. They are also available canned or dried. Substitute button mushrooms or champignons.

### noodles, egg   *ba mee*
Made from eggs and wheat flour, these noodles are the basis of many dishes, stir-fried and in soups. They are used in dishes with a Burmese influence which are very popular in Northern Thailand. Readily available in packets in Western countries, often coiled into small bundles.

To cook, immerse bundles of noodles in a bowl of warm water and let them soak and loosen while a pot of water is put on to boil. Drain the noodles, drop them into the boiling water and cook for 2 or 3 minutes, testing every 30 seconds, until tender but not mushy. Drain well in a colander.

### noodles, rice   *kway teo*
Rice noodles are the most popular variety in Thailand, and there are special noodle shops where fresh rice noodles are produced each day. They are very cheap to buy, and some shops have a 'happy hour' during which all noodles are sold at half price.

Dried rice noodles, which are readily available in supermarkets and grocery stores, come in a variety of thicknesses (*see also* vermicelli, rice). The finest rice vermicelli needs only to be soaked in hot tap water for about 10 minutes, or dropped into boiling water for 1 or 2 minutes. Flatter and thicker rice sticks need soaking in boiling water for 10 minutes.

### noodles, transparent   *woon sen*
Transparent noodles are made from mung bean starch and are very popular in Thailand. They are also called bean starch vermicelli or cellophane noodles. Because these noodles are extremely tough and difficult to cut when dry, I suggest you buy them in small bundles rather than large ones. But if you do have to cut off a small amount, sharp scissors work better than a knife. Soak in hot water or boil as required in individual recipes before using. These noodles will keep indefinitely.

### oil, peanut
Peanut oil processed in the Western way has been refined and deodorised to the point where it has very little, if any, aroma and flavour. Oriental peanut oil, on the other hand, has a definite smell and taste of peanuts and is worth seeking out at Asian stores. If it seems a bit

strong, make a blend of half unrefined and half refined peanut oil.

## palm sugar  *nam tan peep*
Palm sugar comes from boiling down the sweet sap of coconut palms and palmyra palms. It can range from golden to dark brown, and while some of it is solid, in cakes, it is usually sold in jars and has the consistency of brown sugar mixed with treacle. Dark brown sugar makes a reasonable substitute.

## pandanus (screwpine)  *bai toey*
The long, flat, fragrant green leaves of *Pandanus latifolia* are crushed and used as flavouring and colouring in Thai sweets and sweet drinks or simmered with rice to impart their fragrance. The fresh leaves are also fashioned into tiny containers for sweets or wrapped around chicken before it is fried. The leaves are sold fresh, frozen or dried.

It is also possible to buy flavouring essence or paste made from pandanus leaves, the Asian equivalent of vanilla. This is most commonly labelled with its Malaysian name, *pandan*.

## pawpaw, (papaya) green  *malakaw*
Unripe pawpaws (*Carica papaya*) are pale green on the inside. Used to make a very popular *yum* or salad called *Som Tam*.

## pepper  *prik thai*
In Thailand, black pepper (*Piper nigrum*) is one of the primary spices. In fact, though chillies are so entrenched in Thai food, it seems that pepper was used long before chillies were introduced around the sixteenth century. Green peppercorns are also used in Thai cooking, and may be tossed into dishes for extra flavour.

## pickled garlic  *see garlic*

## rice, black sticky  *khao niew*
This is used only in sweets and has a chewy texture. Soak overnight before using.

## rice, glutinous  *khao niew*
In Northern Thailand, as in its neighbouring countries, sticky or glutinous rice is popular, and used mainly in sweet snacks. For plain steamed sticky rice, soak the rice in cold water overnight and drain. Spread in a perforated steamer and steam over boiling water for 30 minutes, turning the rice over halfway through. For a richer result, add 1 cup (8 fl oz) of hot coconut milk to the steamed rice and leave, covered, for a further 30 minutes to absorb the milk. Reheat in the steamer.

## rice, jasmine  *khao chao*
There are many varieties of rice used in Thailand. The kind most favoured as the mainstay of Thai meals is white, long-grained rice with the faint scent of jasmine which occurs naturally. For cooking instructions see page 168.

## sago  *sa-ku*
The starch obtained from the sago palm and other plants with a starchy pith. It looks like little white pearls which, when cooked, becomes clear. Used in both savoury and sweet dishes.

## sesame seeds  *nga*
These nutritious (*Sesamum indicum*) seeds are used mainly for flavouring sweets (usually lightly roasted and ground). White sesame seeds are preferable to black sesame or unhulled seeds. Available at Asian and health food stores.

## shallots  *hom lek*
Shallots (*Allium ascalonicum*) are small, golden brown, purplish or grey bulbs growing in clusters like garlic. They are not slender white bulbs with green tops though, especially in Australia, this is a common mistake. (These are spring onions or scallions.) Shallots are an important ingredient in Thai cooking, but because they are sometimes hard to find, white or brown onions or spring onions may be substituted.

When *crisp-fried shallots* or onions are needed for a recipe, buy them already fried in a packet or tub to save yourself time and trouble. Store in the freezer to keep them from going rancid. If you do not have access to Asian grocery stores, substitute dried onions which can be fried in a little oil. Remove as soon as they turn slightly deeper coloured, and drain on absorbent paper.

### shrimp, dried   *goong haeng*

Dried shrimp are sold in plastic packets in Asian stores. A good way to judge the quality is by the colour, which should be salmon pink, and by pressing the shrimps through the packet – they should yield slightly and not be hard. Above all, they should not smell strongly of ammonia. Keep the packets refrigerated. If they develop a strong or unpleasant smell after long storage, rinse them well in warm water and leave to dry. Dried shrimps will keep for quite a long time but if they start to disintegrate and become powdery, throw them out.

### shrimp paste   *kapi*

When small shrimps are salted and dried in the sun, the liquid which they give off is bottled and matured to make *nam pla*, and the residue goes to make shrimp paste. Pungent enough to warrant being enclosed in a screw-topped bottle, it needs no refrigeration. Use Chinese shrimp sauce or Malaysian *blacan* or anchovy paste as substitutes.

### spring onions (scallions)   *ton hom*

Spring onions are the thinnings of either *Allium cepa* or *A. fistulosum*, plantings that do not form a bulb. Strangely, in Australia these are mistakenly known as shallots.

### tamarind   *ma kham*

Tamarind (*Tamarindus indica*) is a tropical tree which bears long beans with brittle brown shells containing large, hard seeds. The seeds are surrounded by a sweetish-sour brown pulp with a distinctive acid flavour quite different to lemon juice or vinegar.

Tamarind may be purchased in various forms. It may be dried together with the seeds and fibres, only the shell being removed. Or it may be dried without the seeds. If using *dried tamarind*, take a piece the size of a walnut and soak in ½ cup (4 fl oz) of hot water for 10 minutes. Knead and rub with your fingers until the pulp dissolves in the water, and then strain out the seeds and fibres. This is what I refer to as *tamarind liquid*.

One may also purchase *tamarind pulp*. The one I like to use is about as thick as plum sauce – a heavy pouring consistency. Two tablespoons of tamarind pulp concentrate is equal to 1 rounded tablespoon of the dried tamarind that has been soaked.

### *tempeh*

A fermented cake made from soybeans, this features as the 'new health food' and supplies first-class protein in vegetarian meals. Firmer and more flavourful than tofu or bean curd, it is worth investigating.

### turmeric   *kha-min*

A bright yellow rhizome (*Curcuma longa*) from which the familiar yellow powder, the mainstay of cheap curry powders, is obtained. In Thailand most turmeric is used fresh.

### vermicelli, rice   *sen mee*

The finest variety of rice noodles, these are usually ready to serve after soaking in boiling water. They may also be dropped straight into boiling water for a minute or into boiling oil for a few seconds as for *Mee Grob* (*page 179*). They increase in size dramatically, so fry only a small handful at a time and remove from the oil to drain on absorbent paper. The *mee* should puff and swell within seconds, otherwise it means the oil is not hot enough.

### water chestnut   *haeo*

Crisp, slightly sweet, off-white within a dark brownish-black skin that must be peeled off before using, the so-called chestnut (*Eleocharis tuberosa*) is not a nut at all, but the tuber of a sedge. It is used in savoury as well as sweet dishes and is prized for its crisp texture which is retained even through cooking. More readily available canned than fresh.

### wood fungus   *see* black fungus

### white glutinous rice   *see* rice

# INDEX

**NOTE** *Numerals in bold indicate
colour plates*